FACING TODAY'S DEMANDS

FACING TODAY'S DEMANDS

Joseph D. Ban

Judson Press, Valley Forge

FACING TODAY'S DEMANDS

Standard Book No. 8170-0456-4
Library of Congress Catalog Card No. 72-91243

Printed in the U.S.A.

FOREWORD

To relate God's lively Word to the living situation of one's day: such is the task of the interpreter. Whether he teaches or preaches, the Christian spokesman tries to relate the Good News to man's contemporary condition.

These Bible studies on current issues reflect my own involvement as campus pastor and college professor. You will find evidence here that my students press me to "tell it like it is." You will find that my Christian faith forces me to express what "it" can be like in Him.

Three of the chapters were prepared for presentation to the Oregon Baptist Women's conference. They appeared in a small edition published by Linfield College. Five of the studies were presented to the Laity Conference held at the American Baptist Assembly, Green Lake, Wisconsin. I appreciate the response which has encouraged the preparation of this book. "Bridging the Generation Gap" first appeared in print in *The Pulpit,* May, 1968, and is reprinted by permission of the Christian Century Foundation (copyright 1968).

I express appreciation to the President, faculty, and staff of Linfield College, who encourage me in my work as chaplain and whose lives demonstrate the very real possibilities of a Christian style of life in a modern, technological society.

My wife, Arline, co-author on several projects, has encouraged me in my hours given to study and in my honest efforts to blurt out the Good News as best I can. Our children, Sue, Dave, and Debbie, have contributed their insights from their busy lives and given generously in loving support.

JOSEPH D. BAN

Linfield College
McMinnville, Oregon

CONTENTS

1

FACING TODAY'S DEMANDS

Acts 11:1-18

The apostles and the brothers throughout all of Judea heard that the
Gentiles also had received the word of God. [2]When Peter went up to
Jerusalem, those who were in favor of circumcising Gentiles criticized him:
[3]"You were a guest in the home of uncircumcised Gentiles, and you even ate
with them!" [4]So Peter gave them a full account of what had happened,
from the very beginning:

[5]"I was praying in the city of Joppa, and I had a vision. I saw something
coming down that looked like a large sheet being lowered by its four corners from heaven, and it stopped next to me. [6]I looked closely inside and
saw four-footed animals, and beasts, and reptiles, and wild birds. [7]Then
I heard a voice saying to me, 'Get up, Peter; kill and eat!' [8]But I said,
'Certainly not, Lord! No defiled or unclean food has ever entered my
mouth.' [9]The voice spoke again from heaven, 'Do not consider anything
unclean that God has declared clean.' [10]This happened three times, and
finally the whole thing was drawn back up into heaven. [11]At that very
moment three men who had been sent to me from Caesarea arrived at the
house where I was staying. [12]The Spirit told me to go with them without
hesitation. These six brothers also went with me to Caesarea, and we all
went into the house of Cornelius. [13]He told us how he had seen an angel
standing in his house who said to him, 'Send someone to Joppa to call for
a man whose full name is Simon Peter. [14]He will speak words to you by
which you and all your family will be saved.' [15]And when I began to speak,
the Holy Spirit came down on them just as on us at the beginning. [16]Then I
remembered what the Lord had said: 'John baptized with water, but you
will be baptized with the Holy Spirit.' [17]It is clear that God gave those
Gentiles the same gift that he gave us when we believed in the Lord Jesus
Christ; who was I, then, to try to stop God!" [18]When they heard this, they
stopped their criticism and praised God, saying, "Then God has given to
the Gentiles also the opportunity to repent and live!"

Have you noticed of late that few individuals ask for anything? Instead, increasingly, persons and groups make demands. For example, congressional leaders once entertained visitors who came hat in hand. Now congressmen are confronted by hostile delegations who present long lists of demands.

Along with many others, I have experienced great difficulty adjusting to demands. Recently, I left the college campus where I teach to attend the annual meeting of my denomination. I took with me an acute awareness that a responsible group of students had placed before the faculty and administration a series of demands. These were all worthy of attention and deserving of immediate action, but I knew how difficult it was for some professors and administrators to accept demands. They were more accustomed to giving consideration to requests: quietly receiving demands from students was certainly not the usual way of doing things. While this experience was fresh in my thinking, reinforced by a four-hour, airborne conversation with a Negro college administrator, I arrived in the convention city. Lo and behold, a group of black churchmen had presented a series of demands to my denomination!

Some of the denominational leaders and delegates, particularly persons from predominately rural states or states without large minority groups, responded instantly, "Demands! Who are they to demand? Let them ask like everybody else!"

Happily, wiser and more experienced leadership prevailed. Men who have spent long, tiring months patiently trying to translate demands into dignity spoke up. They said: "These are reasonable demands. Let us hear them. These people have been waiting more than a hundred years to speak. But we've been so busy reassuring them that we're their white friends who understand them that we haven't stopped talking long enough to hear what they have to say. Now let's *hear* their demands. Then let's do something about these demands."

My first reaction was not unlike that of some of those who resented demands. While I understood the mood of my own seminary classmates who were black, I had some reservations about the politics and timing of their actions. Then, as I reflected on the total experience, I came to the realization that I should thank the black churchmen, the Linfield students, the poor, for making lists of *demands*. For I began to see that all of us are living in a time best described as the age of demand.

We are living in a time when people have stopped asking and have started demanding. The poor demand that an affluent society let them share in the credit card society. The blacks demand that the whites share their long-hoarded power. The young demand that their elders let loose of some of the handles of social control.

When I relate my experience to Peter's encounter with demands of his day, I see that the *demands* of our day are primary clues to God's purpose for today's Christian and the world. God is making his will known to us in the demands of the poor, the demands of the blacks, the demands of the students in Paris, in Prague, and in McMinnville, Oregon.

For hasn't *demand* characterized God's way of dealing with man? Moses came before Pharoah with demands. Nathan came to King David with demands. The prophet Amos came to the royal shrine at Bethel with demands. Jeremiah confronted the authorities of his day with demands. And what did Jesus do when he came into the temple area set apart for Gentiles and found it sectioned off into concession booths? Did he file a request or enter a petition? No. He not only demanded changes, but he also took action. Of course, Jesus recognized also the price of such decisive action and was ready to pay it in full.

Consider the experience of the apostle Peter as related in Acts 11:1-18. Peter had heeded the urgent request of the Roman centurion Cornelius to come and tell more about God's saving act in Jesus Christ. Peter believed that this request was a demand God had made of him. He not only responded to the invitation to come and interpret the Christian good news, but, to the great horror of his fellow churchmen, he also entered the home of Cornelius and sat down to a meal with this Roman military officer. Then the Jewish Christians confronted Peter with this charge: "You were a guest in the home of uncircumcised Gentiles, and you even ate with them" (Acts 11:3, TEV). Peter recognized the problem of the counterdemand of his fellow Jews. So from Peter's own experience we discover that rarely in life are there *demands without, at the same time, counterdemands.*

Side by side with many present-day demands are equally pressing counterdemands. The poor demand better housing; at the same time, the more affluent demand higher interest rates on funds which could finance home loans.

People appalled by the assassinations of John F. Kennedy, Martin Luther King, Jr., and Robert F. Kennedy demand tighter gun laws, but the National Rifle Association, with its own understanding of constitutional rights, demands that no further restrictions be made upon the sale of firearms.

Life is like that, as many of us can testify. When a man's wife reminds him, "Be sure you get home early today because you promised to put up the basketball backboard for your son," he can be sure that his boss will announce, "Say, today's the day we tackle that big job that's been waiting so long." Demands seem to produce counterdemands.

Some years ago I lived in a suburban community outside of New York City. A society matron visited my wife and me to share a problem. The previous year she had visited in a nation in Africa. Through college connections of her son, she had been the guest in the home of that nation's prime minister. She had had the time of her life. Now that prime minister and his wife were coming to attend some meetings of the United Nations in New York. So our friend wanted to have them as her guests in her home. What was her problem, we asked. "Can you imagine what my neighbors would think if they saw a black couple come up my walk? And stay for dinner?"

Here was a person faced with the demands of social courtesy – to return the hospitality she had so much enjoyed while visiting the African capital – but also sensitive to the counterdemand of her white neighbors.

In Peter's case, word that he had been in Cornelius' house reached Jerusalem long before Peter returned, and his fellow church members were upset, for though they were Christian, their ways of thinking and of doing things were still Jewish. And the Jews would have no personal or social dealings with unclean Gentiles. Peter's defense shows how reluctant the first Christians were to appreciate that the religion of Jesus was like new wine which could not be contained within old wineskins.

We can learn more from Peter's experience with demands which may help us with our living. How did Peter reconcile his new experience with his old tradition? Obviously, Peter's experience was traumatic. That it was a startling experience which had a lasting effect is evident from the dream that he had. For a Jew who thought of himself as fairly orthodox, for a stubborn fisherman, the dream was a shocker. He saw all kinds of things, clean and unclean, in that dream, and then, because Peter was reluctant to accept the unclean items, three different times there came the demand: "Do not consider anything unclean that God has declared clean" (Acts 11:9, TEV). If God is at work in this world, and if God's work may be reflected in events of our times, then we will need to reexamine some of our traditions, our habits, and our patterns to see whether or not we consider unclean those things God has declared clean. When I asked a friend, "What are some of the things we today consider unclean which God may be declaring clean?" his instant response was, "Hippies." Many such young persons are deeply involved in peace movements. They demand that their nation confront the consequences of war and aggression. A Baptist pastor visited among such "peaceniks" and reported to his congregation that, while he did not agree with everything he heard and saw, he did feel the moving of a contagious spirit. He was convinced that we need to be open to the ideas and concerns of these young people who often are characterized as hippies.

Let me describe my own visit to a peace center at Arlington Street Church in Boston, Massachusetts, which has been the scene of the reenactment in modern times of the idea of "sanctuary" that comes from the Middle Ages and earlier. This term defines a place where the civil powers are stayed from executing their will because their intended victim has fled into the divine precincts. In the modern form of sanctuary, young men who call themselves "draft protesters," but who are called "draft dodgers" in newspapers, have sought asylum at the altar of this church. In the Arlington Street Church I talked to a young woman who was identified with the Resistance movement. Note that the name of this protest group is like that of the French underground during the years of Nazi occupation. Their symbol is the Greek letter Omega, the electrical term which stands for resistance. As she described what she had found in the movement, I realized that this was far more than a protest against established society. She spoke of the sense of family, of belonging, of an accepting community of which she is a part. I then said to her, "Pardon me for transferring any of my meanings to your experience, but what you have just said is what I have experienced and hope to experience again in the church. We talk about fellowship, *koinonia,* community."

Her open response was, "We've talked about that, too. We think it funny that people should be denouncing us as radicals and subversives when we're really doing what you're always talking about."

Now I am not certain that God is expressing his will through the resistance movement. However, these young people reject the society and the government which puts on trial the pacifists who have stated their case openly before vast crowds and charges with conspiracy such men as Dr. Benjamin Spock and Chaplain William Sloane Coffin. Young men who have just passed seventeen are refusing to let old men dictate their lives, their destinies, and their deaths. I cannot say precisely that in this matter Peter's experience is saying to us, "Do not declare anything unclean that God has declared clean." All I can say is that we must be aware of the possibility that God may speak to us through these movements.

My trip to Boston was a sobering experience in many ways. We have become aware that every summer is filled with tensions between groups which may explode into violence. Even though I had read a great deal about the alienation of minorities, the reality of this did not strike me until I saw it for myself. At a meeting of hundreds of ministers the day before Memorial Day, we sang together a medley of patriotic hymns, such as "America the Beautiful" and "My Country! 'Tis of Thee." Do you know that almost to a man the black pastors in the group refused to sing any of those patriotic songs? I was shocked. These were my fellow pastors. These were men with whom I had attended seminary. Some of them had been in my home and I in theirs. They were former army chaplains, former servicemen. So deep is the black disillusionment with white society that they can no longer sing the praises of their native land.

Are there some things we have deemed unclean which God declares to be clean? Or have we made unclean some things God always considered clean? Has our white society, by its arrogance, its reluctance to change, and its deep hostilities, effectively foreclosed the possibility of "one nation under God, indivisible, with liberty and justice for all"?

Peter could not bring himself to oppose the demands of God. Not even his enemies in the Sanhedrin wished to come into opposition with God (Acts 5:34-40). Consequently, Peter pleaded with the early church, in effect: "God gave those Gentiles the same gift that he gave us when we put our trust in the Lord Jesus Christ; then how could I possibly stand in God's way?"

Thus, another insight we may gain from Peter's experience is "Trust in the Lord, and get out of God's way." We've seen in Peter that demand evokes counterdemand, and then, that one cannot hold onto what has always seemed to be true if God insists on declaring something new; and now we have this double-edged thrust: *Trust in Jesus Christ — and get out of God's way.*

That truth is not as contradictory as it first appears. For if we really trust in Jesus Christ, we'll not want to stand in God's way. Rather, we will desire to move with him.

During the Reformation in England, the Presbyterian majority in the English Parliament made demands on the English sovereign. Henry, Edward, Mary, and Elizabeth had simple and direct counterdemands: "Off with their heads." This threat did not diminish the demands of the Presbyterian divines. Then the sovereigns became more subtle. They tried a stratagem which has been employed many times since by dissident congregations. "Well, preacher, if you won't preach what we want you to preach, we'll just take away your job." This approach didn't work any more effectively then than it has since. When it was first tried, three hundred clergymen walked off the job. When it was tried next, some years later, two thousand Puritans left their parishes rather than accept the king's command. Somehow they managed to feed their families and to keep their faith alive. They kept their faith, and eventually the government granted freedom of worship to the English people.

In summary, I have shared some of my own doubts and anxieties about today's demands. When I first faced these demands, I reacted negatively. Then my eyes opened to see that the demands of students, of black churchmen, and of peace protesters were a good thing, for these dissidents were bringing into focus the demands of our age. They were forcing me to face up to demands of this day.

From demand to counterdemand I went, feeling sometimes like a birdie shuttling back and forth in a badminton game. Then the recognition came that God may be declaring new things in this new day, and I need to be aware of them. Who am I to consider anything unclean that God has declared clean? Then, sustained by my own experience of prayer, meditation, private reflection, and conversation with others — I have trusted in Jesus and tried to get out of God's way. Who am I to try to stop God!

2
MAKING CRUCIAL DECISIONS

Matthew 15:21-28

21 Jesus left that place and went off to the territory near the cities of Tyre
and Sidon. 22 A Canaanite woman who lived in that region came to him.
"Son of David, sir!" she cried. "Have mercy on me! My daughter has a
demon and is in a terrible condition." 23 But Jesus did not say a word to
her. His disciples came to him and begged him, "Send her away! She is
following us and making all this noise!" 24 Then Jesus replied, "I have been
sent only to the lost sheep of the people of Israel." 25 At this the woman
came and fell at his feet. "Help me, sir!" she said. 26 Jesus answered, "It
isn't right to take the children's food and throw it to the dogs." 27 "That is
true sir," she answered; "but even the dogs eat the leftovers that fall from
their masters' table." 28 So Jesus answered her: "You are a woman of great
faith! What you want will be done for you." And at that very moment her
daughter was healed.

Although the meaning and value of my own life have been shaped by my personal knowledge of Jesus Christ as Lord and Savior, I cannot accept the assumption of many that the life of Jesus was simply a great big success story. The Christian church has always insisted that Jesus was a man, a human person. Thus, he had to face the agony of making crucial decisions by the very human process of trial and error. He had to use the same tools which you and I have to use – namely, reflection and reason.

Let us look at one very difficult decision which Jesus had to make. As we examine this experience in his life, we will also be reflecting on our own life situation. We will be looking at Jesus' encounter with one stubborn Canaanite woman and asking three questions: First, what persistent life issue is evidenced in this experience? Second, how did the religious tradition help or hinder Jesus in his decision making? Third, where did Jesus' need and his religious faith intersect, and how did that crossing point take place? The term "crossing point" has been adopted by Christian educators to identify the point at which the specific needs of a person in a particular situation and his Christian faith intersect and where crucial decisions must be made.

Let us begin with the first question: What is the persistent life issue? Recall some event which has altered the course of your life. Think of some particular instance when you personally underwent some real change. Such a life-affecting encounter can happen almost anywhere at any time. Often enough such an experience comes at some point of concern. There are some concerns that stick with us through all of life. When just now you began reflecting on some life-altering experience of your own, did the experience that came to your mind have anything to do with a persistent life issue? Some questions stay with us through the years, such as: Who am I? What kind of person am I? Why am I here? What should I be doing with my life? What is "my thing"? What is the meaning of my sexuality? Questions like these engage our concern whether we are fifteen or fifty years old. Questions of life purpose, of life pursuits, of life partners, of life philosophy – such *persistent life issues* are usually the places at which life's crossing points take place.

Such a persistent life issue may be discerned in Jesus' experience with the stubborn woman of Canaan. The incident occurred as Jesus left his native Galilee and wandered north into the pagan territory of Tyre and Sidon. He was not only looking for some rest but possibly was also escaping the secret police of Herod Antipas. The story suggests that Jesus had some problems which he wanted to sort out. He needed time and he needed quiet for thought and reflection.

The disciples were particularly disturbed by this noisy, insistent woman. They came and begged Jesus: "Do send her away! Just look at how she comes shouting after us."

Jesus' reply was made to the disciples, but the interested woman also heard him say: "I have been sent only to the lost sheep of the people of Israel" (Matthew 15:24, TEV).

Those words of Jesus define one of his own persistent life issues. Jesus seems to be asking: "What really is my mission? Here I am, a wandering rabbi, driven to this life because I have a vision of what God's kingly rule is all about. What does my concept of my mission in life have to do with this heathen woman? I thought I had it all sorted out after the experience of the temptations. I thought then that I was pretty clear about what I was going to teach. Certainly the experience at my baptism had confirmed me in knowing that I was to invest my life in urging God's kingdom upon my fellow Jews. But what does this *noisy*, stubborn woman have to do with my mission in life?"

What kind of ministry was Jesus to have? This question was a persistent life issue for him. Some of us face questions like: What major shall I declare in college; shall I go into graduate school; what profession shall I choose? Others have to consider questions about a change in occupation; wives and mothers wonder whether to get or keep a job outside the home. All such questions bring to the surface this persistent life issue: What am I to be? What is my purpose in life?

The contemporary Christian martyr, Dr. Martin Luther King, Jr., in his autobiography stated how he faced a similar question, "Shall I go back into the South?" All of his postgraduate education had been in the North. His wife, Coretta, had been educated at Antioch College in Ohio. Being black was handicap enough in the South; but to have been educated in the North doubled the trouble he would face in the South.

The biographies of Richard M. Nixon, Hubert H. Humphrey, and the late Robert F. Kennedy carry some evidences of the personal search of those leaders for answers to these questions: "Just what is it I am supposed to be doing with this one life I have to live? How do I go about conducting myself on this pilgrimage called life?"

I have noticed that men and women who achieve some measure of greatness are aware of this question of purpose. All men sooner or later come up against it. Some face the question openly and manfully. Others face it in the bottom of a bottle or in front of a television set. Man, to be man, must deal rationally with what he has done, what he is doing, and what he is going to do with this span of life that has been measured out to him.

Jesus thought he had his course of action worked out, until this persistent pagan butted into his nicely laid-out plans and began to badger him. She wanted to "cut in on the action."

The disciples responded impulsively and peevishly. Jesus responded thoughtfully but with no less certainty: "But you pagans are not my thing. I have come to the House of Israel." Which is to say: "You Gentiles sweat it out for yourselves."

We come to our second question: How did the religious tradition help or hinder Jesus in his decision making? One's religious faith should be of help when it comes to dealing with persistent life issues. But religion doesn't always aid us. Certainly Jewish traditions and leaders had failed Jesus.

His religious instructors had failed him in the attitudes which they had taught him about women. Women were second-class citizens, necessary nuisances at best. Actually, Jesus had to overcome a good deal of mis-instruction even to carry on a meaningful dialogue with a woman. Mary, the mother of Jesus, must have been an unusually gifted woman in that she could help her son to see past the prejudices against women built into the religious institution of his day. If anything characterizes the American male, it is a similar inability to accept the true being of a woman. Modern men tend to "use" women. Few males are able to relate fully to the humanity of the female.

A more severe handicap which Jesus faced was the attitude of the traditional Jewish religion against outsiders. When the Jews returned from exile, they found it necessary to insist on purity of the race. This intolerant attitude did help Judaism to survive, but it also limited Jewish understanding of God. Now Jesus wrestled with the questions: "Is God the Lord of the Jew and the male only? Or does God have a concern for pagans and for women? Is it right to take the children's food and throw it to the puppies?"

Not only had Jesus' religious instructors failed him, but today's Christian educators may be guilty similarly of heaping burdens unnecessarily upon the persons who come for instruction. For example, incessant talking *about* God has obscured the possibility of persons experiencing God. Or again, we too often talk of the kingdom of God as if it were identical with the organized church. We equate the words "ministers" and "ministry" with whatever is necessary to keep the institution going, and thus we totally miss the responsibility each one of us has to minister in the world as Jesus did.

But Jesus did come to a crossing point. He did open up and allow this pagan's plea to get through to him: "Even the dogs eat the leftovers that fall from their masters' table" (Matthew 15:27, TEV). Despite the failure of the synagogue of his day and the churches of our day, some truth is still getting across in the process of religious instruction. Jesus had been instructed in the prophets, and he knew that, from Isaiah to Ezekiel, the prophets had witnessed to God as Lord over all mankind. So the very religious system which gave Jesus so much of the wrong information also equipped him to make an appropriate response when he came to his moment of decision.

The church that is supposed to help us to deal adequately with life's crossing points doesn't always come through. Yet despite the failures, where modern Christian men and women do make an appropriate response to life, the foundation has been laid in all that was, and was not, communicated by the process of Christian education.

So now we come to the third, last, and most important question: Where did Jesus' need and his religious faith intersect? Old Testament prophets such as Amos had insisted that the treatment of women and children, widows and orphans, was the test of a nation. Other prophets had emphasized that Israel's God was sovereign over all the nations of mankind. This emphasis was part of Jesus' religious heritage.

The persistent life issue which emerged for him in this encounter with the Canaanite woman was the question: What is my "thing" in life? What am I supposed to be doing?

For Jesus, when his faith and his experience intersected, a crossing point emerged. Using the insights of his religious heritage to illuminate his present predicament, he decided to break with the past and grant to the woman the request for which she was pleading. "You are a woman of great faith! What you want will be done for you" (Matthew 15:28, TEV).

For Jesus, the cries and pleas of this persistent pagan woman permitted him to break away from the old patterns imposed by his religious instructors and allowed him to discover in a new way that God is sovereign over all men: He is not just the God of the Jews or just the God of the faithful few.

Where God's truth breaks through and transforms our human

experience, there is the crossing point. Where are the possible crossing points in our own lives? Some young man may be saying, "I want to be patriotic; I love my country but I cannot kill." Or someone traversing those decades between the thirties and the sixties, which I like to call "the creative years," may someday say: "I've worked awfully hard for that promotion, but I just cannot make it." What does the Christian gospel have to say for such problems? What can we affirm about the value of human life compared to the love of country; about the dignity of human life that is more than five-figure salaries; about why we are here in human flesh?

The crossing point occurs wherever God speaks to us in our human situation and wherever God moves us to act.

Note that there are many possible crossing points in a lifetime. Because the issues do persist all through life and because the gospel speaks *to* all of life, crossing points can emerge in many different ways.

Some are bridges which we will have to cross almost every day. Such decisions are probably no less crossing points, but they have lesser consequences, at least in the short run, because we have the opportunity to rectify wrong choices. But other crossing points are akin to burning our bridges behind us.

The encounter that Jesus had with the Canaanite woman was one such crucial decision. In both Matthew's and Mark's accounts, just before this incident Jesus had been warning his disciples about the false advice of the Pharisees. What he had been saying in words, he had to translate into deeds. He recognized that he himself had been lost in the fog of Pharisaism, but found his direction. The Canaanite mother had her desire granted; her child was healed. His crossing point behind him, Jesus headed for Jerusalem.

When we face crucial decisions, crossing points in our lives, we need to try to identify the persistent life issue that is at the heart of the problem. Then we must ask how our religious heritage helps or hinders us in making a decision. When a persistent life issue and our religious faith intersect, we are at the crossing point from which we may launch out in new directions.

3
HAPPENING OR HOLY SPIRIT

Acts 11:19-26

19The believers were scattered by the persecution which took place when
Stephen was killed. Some of them went as far as Phoenicia and Cyprus and
Antioch, telling the message to Jews only. 20But some of the believers, men
from Cyprus and Cyrene, went to Antioch and told the message to Gentiles
also, preaching to them the Good News about the Lord Jesus. 21The Lord's
power was with them, and a great number of people believed and turned
to the Lord.

22The news about this reached the church in Jerusalem, so they sent
Barnabas to Antioch. 23When he arrived and saw how God had blessed
the people, he was glad and urged them all to be faithful and true to the
Lord with all their hearts. 24Barnabas was a good man, full of the Holy
Spirit and faith. Many people were brought to the Lord.

25Then Barnabas went to Tarsus to look for Saul. 26When he found him,
he brought him to Antioch. For a whole year the two met with the people
of the church and taught a large group. It was at Antioch that the disciples
were first called Christians.

From New York's Central Park to San Francisco's Golden Gate Park, all of America is interested in a "happening." Indeed, happenings are so popular that now you can purchase a ticket for an "off-Broadway" theater and see well-publicized, oft-rehearsed happenings. The word "happening" describes an event characterized by spontaneous, eager, often joyous activity. "Whatever happens" is what makes a happening. When I was reading about the primitive Christian church and the unexpected turns in its early history, I came upon this phrase: "Nevertheless events, or rather God's Holy Spirit." Because the word "event" for me conveys the meaning that the word "happening" seems to communicate to young moderns, my mind instantly translated "events or the Holy Spirit" into "happening or Holy Spirit." Are there some events or happenings in our lifetime which are really the action of God's Holy Spirit? Let's see what the happenings in the lives of those early Christians may say about the Holy Spirit's activity in our own lives. When we read Acts 11:19-26, we find that God's happenings take place in unlikely places, using unlikely means, and employing unlikely men.

If we learn anything from the life of the early church, we learn that God chooses the most *unlikely places* for a happening. If those early Christians could have had modern management consultants directing their enlistment campaign, they would have been warned to stay away from Antioch. A modern public relations counselor would have told them: "Avoid Antioch. It's a hopeless situation. If you want to start a clean-cut business, such as a church, get a nice community where there are steady people. Homeowners who love kids; that's what you want."

Antioch was the sin city of the Mediterranean world. The patron god of Antioch was Tyche, the god of fortune. The city had an international reputation for chariot racing and was widely known for the deliberate pursuit of pleasure, which continued around the clock, day and night.

Ancient writers were unanimous in describing cosmopolitan Antioch as one of the most depraved cities in the world. Every fierce and base passion was displayed by the populace – licentiousness, superstition, and quackery. They were notoriously skilled in coining scurrilous verses. The sordid, fickle, turbulent, and insolent ways of the people had turned the name of Antioch into a byword for all that is unclean.

Isn't that enough to warn any Christian organization to keep away? Not much chance of getting a foothold in that unlikely place. Antioch may have been an unlikely place, but it was not an ungodly place. The people had their gods, all right, in Antioch. As well as Tyche, they had Daphne and Apollo. Because of Daphne and Apollo the people of Antioch had a shameless disregard for the principles of morality. Daphne was once a local girl, rather pretty. Apollo was the handsome god from Mount Olympus who came and fell in love with her. The residents of Antioch at first told stories of how Apollo chased Daphne through the woods. Then the people built the Groves of Daphne. Ten miles in circumference, the groves contained waterfalls, cypress trees, and beautiful gardens. This park was filled with shrines to Apollo, Venus, Isis – all of them fertility gods. It was crowded with theaters, baths, taverns, and dance halls. The Groves of Daphne became a huge pleasure area where abominable sex practices were carried on in the name of religion, for the priestesses were sacred prostitutes. So infamous were these groves that any soldier of the Imperial Roman Army who was detected there was not only punished but dismissed from the imperial service.

Surely this city was a most unlikely place for the Christian church to begin a new enterprise. Never was there a more unpromising place for one of God's happenings than Antioch. Yet in Antioch the early believers gathered, set to work, taught, prayed, sang, worshiped – and their numbers grew. Indeed, at Antioch they were first called Christians.

If there is anything we can learn from their experience, it is that *there is no such thing as a hopeless situation.* That lesson is needed because some persons have felt rather desperate about the provincial-mindedness of America's small towns. An instance is the case of a man who had virtually concluded a transaction to sell his home in a small town just about the time of a local election at which a school tax levy came before the voters. When the levy was defeated, the prospective buyer withdrew his offer, stating that he did not want to live in a community which refused to provide quality education. In another case, a man in one of the professions seriously considered moving to a more urban center because of the bigotry and provincial mentality he had discovered in a small town. I have found something of the same despair among college students. They are very much aware that things are happening in that great big world outside, but they feel that they are a part of what seems to be a little, conservative state where life moves at a snail's pace.

Because of such criticisms, I want to underscore my conviction that God creates happenings in the most unlikely places. My small town of McMinnville is as unlikely a place for a happening of the Holy Spirit as any other town of nine thousand inhabitants. But in just such a place one of God's happenings may take place. How big was Wittenberg, Germany, when Luther nailed his ninety-five theses to the door of the castle church? Everybody had heard of Rome. Who had heard of Wittenberg? Or what about Nazareth? Who had ever heard of Nazareth? It was such a joke that anything good might ever come out of Nazareth that there was even a saying about it. Nazareth, Antioch, Wittenberg, McMinnville – God can make unlikely places the scenes of real happenings.

Not only does God make things happen in unlikely places; he

also uses *unlikely means* for his happenings. Many people think that in order for there to be a real miracle, something has to happen in an instant. But God's miracles are not always instantaneous. Note the slow stages, the long, hard pull, before the happening that is described in Acts 11:21. Here for the first time the good news of Jesus Christ was preached to the Gentiles. But at least three slow stages were needed before this happening was possible. First, Philip preached to the Samaritans (Acts 8:4-13). That was the first phase. Then next, Peter accepted Cornelius, the Roman centurion (Acts 10:34-48). But what a long drawn-out affair that event became when Peter had to justify his actions to the Jewish Christian group back in Jerusalem!

For a while it looked as though there would be an "unhappening," with the staunch conservatives undoing all the work of the Holy Spirit. Even in that incident when Cornelius came to the Christians, the Christians did not go out to Cornelius. But the church did move through the painful, deliberate process of phase two and came to phase three. In Antioch the Christians did *not* wait for a seeker to knock on their church door. The Christians deliberately set out, spontaneously and without invitation, to preach the Good News to the Gentiles. After a long, agonizing delay, the Christians launched out on a worldwide mission. That slow, deliberate process, nevertheless, was a miracle. There was nothing instant about it, no fast 10-9-8-7-6-5-4-3-2-1-swoosh – it's off the launching pad. No, some of God's most important happenings take time, lots of time; lots of brutally agonizing, depressingly anxious spending of time; months and years of time.

I know of a Christian home where for years the father had been estranged from the church. His wife and children loved him and appreciated him as a father, but they recognized that his life was incomplete. So the mother and children prayed for him. They didn't feel superior to him, but they felt love and compassion for him. For one year, five years, ten years, twenty years they cared for him as he cared for them; they loved him as he loved them; they prayed for him even though he did not pray for them. Then there came a time when he was able to express his need for Jesus Christ. He confessed his faith in his Savior, asked to be received into the Christian church, and requested baptism. His life now had a sense of fulfillment it had lacked before. His love and his compassion now had new depths. God's most important happenings take lots of time.

If you will read ahead in Acts 19, you will find the Apostle Paul preaching in another city very much like Antioch. Ephesus was also an unlikely place for one of God's happenings. Day after day Paul taught in the synagogue. After three months, what happened? Jewish leaders threw Paul right out of that synagogue. There is one of God's happenings for you. And what did Paul do in that unlikely place of Ephesus? After three months of daily preaching which led to failure and rejection, Paul immediately rented a hall. There in the *siesta hours* from 11:00 A.M. to 4:00 P.M., when no one else would lecture (when any Ephesian with a brain in his head was having his midday nap), that man Paul taught every single day. During the other hours, he worked at his trade for his room and board; for he paid his own way. He taught for five hours and then went back to his sewing and mending of tents. In this fashion Paul preached for *two years.* No instant miracles there but lots of hard work. We, too, may have days when we don't know whether or not the struggle is worth the effort. Discouragement, doubt, dependency on loved ones and friends; patience, sticking to the task, the long, hard pull – that experience, too, is a happening; that, too, is an event; that, too, is God's miracle.

God does use unlikely means to bring about a happening. This fact was true in Antioch and in Ephesus. It is still true in towns and cities today.

Even as God uses unlikely places and unlikely means, he also employs *unlikely men;* for in the midst of a miracle there stands a human person. At the heart of one of God's happenings stands a man or woman.

Now, when Barnabas came to Antioch, he didn't have much to guide him. There were no precedents, no previous experience, no traditions to go by. Coming from Cyprus, he was a Jew from the Dispersion. He was a Levite from the tribe of priests. He had sold his land and donated the proceeds to the early Christian community (Acts 4:36). In that determined group he was often called upon for a judgment, especially when the church had to make a decision on the basis of altogether too few facts. As a consequence, the early church owes much to the wise decisions of Barnabas in the face of difficult problems.

God often must use such men in changing situations, where experience and tradition are liabilities rather than assets. Barnabas was the man who guaranteed to a suspicious church that Paul's conversion was genuine (Acts 9:26-27). This man, whose openness toward others and whose sensitivity had earned him the name "son of encouragement," was once again called upon to make a decision. History now shows his choice of Paul to have been a life-and-death matter in the development of the Christian church. Shouldn't God have directed that a more experienced man be selected? Surely a more prestigious man should have been chosen. Even Barnabas would soon recognize that the situation at Antioch needed the services of a better-trained, more skillful man. We would think that if God insists on bringing about his happenings in such difficult ways, choosing such unlikely spots, using such unlikely means, at least the Holy Spirit should employ the best available man. When there are two out in the last half of the ninth inning and the other team is ahead, even a baseball manager who is a bum knows enough to send in his very best hitter. If there's going to be a happening, then send the best man. That's our wisdom. But God uses someone other than the obvious first choice. Barnabas went, a man who was all heart. William Barclay calls Barnabas "the man with the biggest heart in the Church."[1] Barnabas responded with a glad heart, and he encouraged them. In baseball words, he got to first base. Then, he went to get Paul. Paul stepped to the plate and drove a liner out into centerfield that brought Barnabas all around those bases and safely across homeplate.

[1] William Barclay, *The Acts of the Apostles* (Philadelphia: The Westminster Press, 1957), p. 95.

God has the strangest way of bringing one of his happenings into being – unlikely places, unlikely means, unlikely men.

All the world has known that America is enmeshed in a serious racial problem. Even a Swedish sociologist, Gunnar Myrdal, definitively described the racial situation more than a generation ago. Now, if we are aware of the complexities of the problem, certainly God has known the dimensions of our difficulty. What did He do? In an unlikely place (Montgomery, Alabama, the very birthplace of the Confederacy), using unlikely means (public busses and a tired Negro woman), God took unlikely people (Rosa Parks, some black Baptist preachers, school-age kids, and tired old grandmothers); and out of it all, he fashioned himself a happening. And what a happening!

Who would have imagined, when word got around that all Rosa Parks wanted to do was get off her tired feet, that all the people in the black community would get *on* their feet and start walking to work, bypassing the city busses. Out of the unlikely place of Montgomery, there came the Civil Rights Movement. Out of the unlikely means of a bus boycott, there came the beginning of a new American revolution. Out of the unlikely person of a black preacher, there came a Nobel Prize winner, who became an internationally recognized prophet of justice, of nonviolence, and of concern for the poor of this earth.

We are living in a world marked by social upheavals. The world of the early Christians was similar. In this kind of changing world, we need to look for God's happenings. Unfortunately, where the *divine* is at work, the *demonic* can also be found. So, to the wise and faithful man is given the task of distinguishing between signs of good and signs of evil. For example, the movement for Civil Rights and the awakening of our consciences to the plight of the poor are good, I believe. I honestly can discern signs of the activity of God in these events. But the assassinations of three great Americans (John F. Kennedy, Martin Luther King, Jr., and Robert F. Kennedy) were demonic, I believe. Also, I have the same feeling about housewives in Detroit suburbs arming themselves with pistols and practicing target shooting. Those actions are the signs of evil agencies at work in our time.

You and I, like Barnabas, are called today to make decisions through which God can create a happening. What we say and what we do will lead others to decision and action. We may not have much experience, specialized education, or tradition to guide us, but we must decide and act. Our decision or our indecision will help or hinder others.

Let's take a last look at Barnabas. He was alert enough to realize that God can work in unlikely places like Antioch, using unlikely means, such as the interest and activity of a Roman military officer, and unlikely persons, such as Gentiles in a pagan-pleasure capital, to create a happening.

God makes use of unlikely places, unlikely means, and unlikely men to accomplish his eternal purposes. Do you and I live in an unlikely place? Are the forces of change in our world the unlikely means? Does God have an assignment for such unlikely persons as we are?

Are today's events just happenings or are they God's happenings?

4
INCOMPLETE CHRISTIANS

Acts 19:1-7

While Apollos was in Corinth, Paul traveled through the interior of the
province and arrived in Ephesus. There he found some disciples, [2]and
asked them, "Did you receive the Holy Spirit when you believed?" "We
have not even heard that there is a Holy Spirit," they answered. [3]"Well,
then, what kind of baptism did you receive?" Paul asked. "The baptism of
John," they answered. [4]Paul said: "The baptism of John was for those who
turned from their sins; and he told the people of Israel that they should
believe in the one who was coming after him – that is, in Jesus." [5]When
they heard this, they were baptized in the name of the Lord Jesus. [6]Paul
placed his hands on them, and the Holy Spirit came upon them; they talked
with strange sounds and also spoke God's word. [7]They were about twelve
men in all.

Many people are disturbed because in the fellowship of their churches they have experienced dissension instead of harmony. They have heard some church leaders insist that the church must take a more active role in changing the structures and institutions in our society. At the same time, other leaders, equally sincere and earnest, claim that the only way to have a truly good society is to encourage each individual to develop his own personal relationship with God. The devout person caught between these conflicting claims wonders how both groups can claim so boldly to be serving the same Lord, while they are advocating such different styles of mission.

The people who are disturbed by this tension between personal piety and social concern may find some help by taking another look at an incident in Paul's life (Acts 19:1-7). Paul came to the city of Ephesus and found twelve men who knew of Jesus, had been baptized in John's baptism of repentance, but had not even heard that the Holy Spirit exists. Actually, they were incomplete Christians, for without God's power made real through the Holy Spirit, there is no such thing as complete Christianity.

The Scottish expositor of the Scriptures, William Barclay, catches the right note in this bit of the history of the early church. He does not attempt to determine which of the baptisms, by John or in the name of Jesus, was the correct one. What Barclay does say is that those who knew only the baptism of

John were incomplete Christians, because "they did not know the grace of Christ and the help of the Holy Spirit."[1]

If these twelve men in Ephesus can be called incomplete Christians, then we might term some forms of the Christianity of our time as incomplete. One form of Christianity emphasizes personal piety to the neglect of social concern, and another type is deeply involved in social action to the neglect of personal faith and nurture. Both forms of incomplete Christianity pose a problem for today's church member.

The person who practices his individualistic piety without reference to his neighbor's need is illustrated in John Bunyan's hero in *Pilgrim's Progress.* The man named Christian embarked on an intensely personal pilgrimage for salvation. So great was his desire to reach that goal of salvation, the Celestial City, that he jammed his fists into his ears to shut out the anguished cries of his wife and children who called to him to wait for them.

His many years in prison gave John Bunyan opportunity to think more about the meaning of the Christian faith. In his sequel to *Pilgrim's Progress* the wife and children are included in Christian's pilgrimage toward eternal life. Thus, John Bunyan recognized that man's salvation has a social dimension. I am convinced that were he writing in today's world he would probably write about how Christian set about evangelizing the social apparatus which men create and which, in turn, forms men's lives.

There was the baptism of John, not incorrect, only incomplete. There is personal piety on the one hand and social action on the other. Neither is incorrect; each alone is incomplete.

Piety without social concern is incomplete. Social involvement without the discipline of prayer, Bible study, and worship is incomplete.

The incompleteness of such present-day Christians may be described in this way. The pietists are acquainted personally with the Holy Spirit but are unfamiliar about where he works. The social activists are regularly acquainted with the work of

[1] William Barclay, *The Acts of the Apostles* (Philadelphia: The Westminster Press, 1957), p. 154.

the Holy Spirit, but they are not on a basis of personal acquaintance with him.

Now if there are such forms of incomplete Christianity present today, we must ask: Is there a cure for today's incomplete Christian?

As in Ephesus, so in today's situation, incomplete Christians stand in need of the baptism of the Holy Spirit.

Here allow me to use an idea that comes from both the American evangelist, Billy Graham, and the European churchman, Hans-Ruedi Weber. I first heard the idea presented by World Council staffer, Dr. Weber. Billy Graham later used the same image in an address before the meeting of the National Council of Churches in Miami, Florida. These men spoke of the double conversion, using Paul's view of baptism as burial of the old man in the waters of baptism and the resurrection of the new man from the watery grave. Double conversion begins with the conversion by Jesus Christ of the old man from the pagan, immoral world into the new life in the Christian community. That's the first conversion. Out of the old into the new.

In the second conversion, the new man begins to work with Christ in the yet-to-be-redeemed sectors of human experience. This idea is close to the teachings of Jesus himself. Remember that Jesus promised his followers that the Holy Spirit would come when the disciples would be in the world. We also remember the prayer of Jesus as declared in John's Gospel: "I sent them into the world just as you sent me into the world" (John 17:18, TEV).

The coming of the Holy Spirit is the only known cure for incomplete Christianity. For the forms of incomplete Christianity that can be diagnosed by the symptoms of individualistic piety, on the one hand, and social action without a discipline of renewal, on the other hand, we have suggested double conversion as the cure. The cure for both forms of incomplete Christianity is entry into the new life with Christ in order to follow him into his ministry in the world.

Hans-Ruedi Weber tells how the Christian church got the word "sacrament." (The Lord's Supper and baptism are called sacraments by some Protestant churches and ordinances by others. The earliest Baptist churches in England and America used either term or both terms, sacrament and ordinance, in referring to baptism and the Lord's Supper.) The word "sacrament" comes from the word *sacramentum,* a military oath. In the armies of the far-flung Roman empire, "the decisive act of becoming a soldier was called the *sacramentum.* . . . The Christian Church adopted this word for the decisive act of becoming a soldier of Christ." [2] In baptism, then, we take an oath to enter into the service of our Lord. It is unfortunate that so many of us who have accepted the sacramentum (the baptismal vows) do not actually join in Christ's struggle for the world. After taking their "military oath," many such incomplete Christians actually become deserters, fleeing from their duties and responsibilities. Others seem to take a more or less permanent leave, occasionally returning for a military dress review or a field day. Easter and Christmas are easily recognized among such military exercises. Some of us soldiers remain in the barracks, always polishing our spiritual armor for God, but we never leave the Christian camp to fight for God's purposes of reconciliation for mankind. We never get away from rehearsing our private pieties in order to engage in the fight to rescue the body social and politic from the enslaving and demonic forces destroying it.

Having taken our oath in baptism, let us train and prepare to go out and do battle. The cure for our incomplete Christianity is the double conversion: first, our conversion from the world to Christ, and then, our conversion to service with Christ.

After the incomplete Christians in Ephesus received the Holy Spirit, they spoke with tongues and prophesied. What are some of the modern signs of the presence of the Holy Spirit? What is the effect of a healthy, complete Christianity? In the history of the Christian church we can find many illustrations of those healthier times when piety and social concern were not divorced. Actually, when the pietistic movement began in comparatively recent times, evangelical piety and social work were twins. This

[2] Hans-Ruedi Weber, *Salty Christians* (New York: The Seabury Press, Inc., 1963), p. 25.

is well illustrated in the great figure of German pietism, August Hermann Francke. His life spanned the late seventeenth and early eighteenth centuries. Francke introduced pietism into the University of Halle, which each year graduated two hundred ministers into the churches of Germany.

Many of Francke's students sailed to America to serve Lutheran congregations in the new nation. The king of Denmark turned to Halle when he wanted missionaries to send to Danish outposts around the world. Francke combined evangelical piety with intensive social work. His orphanages and schools set a pattern that was widely imitated.

We can find another example of the fruitful combination of Christian piety and social concern in the evangelical movement of John Wesley in England. The Wesleyan revival proved to be an intensely powerful force in the lives of the people. It has been credited with saving England from the violent disruptions of the French revolution. That such a statement is an accurate historical judgment can be understood by recalling the contributions of Christians like William Wilberforce. A wealthy, popular member of Parliament, he was converted to the evangelical movement in 1784. He felt so intensely about his faith that he wrote a book of more than four hundred pages in length, in which he called others to serious and holy living. Three years after his conversion, he began to fight the socially and legally accepted practice of slavery.

For thousands of years slavery had been present in civilization. The Empires of Alexander, of Rome, of Byzantium, of Charlemagne, plus the Holy Roman Empire and the British Empire, had tolerated traffic in slaves. Could one man put a stop to this profitable and very extensive commercial enterprise? The recent evangelical convert, Wilberforce, began his fight in 1787. Twenty years later, in 1807, he won the abolition of the slave trade in the British dominions. Slavery, itself, was outlawed in 1833. However, in America, not until after the Civil War of 1861-1865 did the United States move to stop the selling and trading of humans, as one sells and trades tools or horses.

Wilberforce was at the same time the pietist and the social

activist. Following his conversion, he "gave up card-playing, denied himself luxuries, distributed a fourth of his wealth to the destitute, and became a student of the Bible. He was typical of men in places of leadership who were directly affected by the evangelical piety of the Methodists." [3]

The lives of two Baptist men in America will illustrate further the fruitful progeny when piety and social action are wed.

Early in this century a German Baptist demonstrated what a socially oriented evangelical can do. As a young pastor working among German immigrants in New York's Hell's Kitchen, Walter Rauschenbusch was so sensitive to the social needs of his people that he even counted, on one occasion, the steps a young mother had to descend and ascend each day to get from her tenement walk-up to work and to the grocery store and back. The sensitive pastor knew each step she took, counted the curbstones she lifted her baby carriage down and up again. Out of this personally intense concern, plus his own personal piety, there grew the awareness of a need for changing the shape of society, so that all men might share in the good things of this earth. From this man's quite conservative theology, there grew a socially oriented gospel that was to redirect America's energies.[4]

The last illustration of men who combine personal piety with social awareness can be drawn from the life of Edwin T. Dahlberg. He was the first pastor of a local congregation ever elected to the presidency of the National Council of Churches. His congregations knew him as an authentic minister of reconciliation. The nation knew him through the front pages of the newspapers, which pictured him in peace marches, civil rights demonstrations, and as a friend and supporter of Martin Luther King, both father and son. He supported many causes, some popular, many unpopular. I personally can testify how much Dr. Dahlberg's Christian life, his devotional and prayer life, have influenced my own. His life is a superb example that the bringing together of

[3] Clyde L. Manschreck, ed., *A History of Christianity,* vol. 2 (Englewood Cliffs, N. J.: Prentice-Hall, Inc., 1964), p. 271.

[4] Dores R. Sharpe, *Walter Rauschenbusch* (New York: The Macmillan Company, 1942), from the introduction by Harry E. Fosdick, p. xii.

personal piety and social concern helps to make one a more complete Christian.

But these are all great men from past generations. Are there not illustrations from the present? I can point to congregations, some quite small, others quite large, where more complete Christians are now in the making. One such congregation has many small groups serving in task forces. These task forces confront contemporary problems, such as poverty and affluence, war and peace, science and religion, and adequate housing for minorities. They study the social problem, even as they study their Bible. They pray about a problem situation, and then they go out and do something about it. Such groups may have Bible study one day and a social action project the next. One such student group was directed by a social worker to help a family on welfare with a sanitary problem. The students, among them some campus co-eds better known for their beauty than their knowledge of sanitary engineering, spent a long eight-hour evening cleaning out an outhouse, bucket after filthy bucket. Said one serious co-ed after this experience, "I learned more in those eight hours than I did in all four years of college." Service of one's fellowmen leads to service of God.

There are many forms of incomplete Christianity in our churches today. Two such forms have been mentioned. Piety without social responsibility is incomplete. Social concern without the disciplines of the faith is also less than complete. When my concern for my fellowmen is undergirded by a personal relationship to God through Jesus Christ, I not only come closer to being more complete as a Christian, I also come closer to serving more completely my fellowman.

Jesus sends us to serve in the world, even as his Father sent him into the world to serve. As we go into the world, we can be assured that the Holy Spirit will support and sustain our efforts. Let's harness both our personal faith and our social responsibility and thus approach a more complete expression of Christian faith.

As a dedicated Roman Catholic woman once said: "My husband and I would like to live the kind of holy life which brings us very close to Christ without separating us from men — to be saints whose daily life is just like that of ordinary people, but so truly human, so radiant with life and joy, so balanced, that one longs to be like them, and in trying to discover what makes them like that, one discovers Christ."

5

COME ALIVE

Romans 8:9-17

9But you do not live as your human nature tells you to; you live as the
Spirit tells you to — if, in fact, God's Spirit lives in you. Whoever does
not have the Spirit of Christ does not belong to him. 10But if Christ lives
in you, although your body is dead because of sin, yet the Spirit is life for
you because you have been put right with God. 11If the Spirit of God, who
raised Jesus from death, lives in you, then he who raised Christ from death
will also give life to your mortal bodies by the presence of his Spirit in you.
12So then, my brothers, we have an obligation, but not to live as our
human nature wants us to. 13For if you live according to your human nature, you are going to die; but if, by the Spirit, you kill your sinful actions,
you will live. 14Those who are led by God's Spirit are God's sons. 15For
the Spirit that God has given you does not make you a slave and cause
you to be afraid; instead, the Spirit makes you God's sons, and by the
Spirit's power we cry to God, "Father! my Father!" 16God's Spirit joins
himself to our spirits to declare that we are God's children. 17Since we are
his children, we will possess the blessings he keeps for his people, and we
will also possess with Christ what God has kept for him; for if we share
Christ's suffering, we will also share his glory.

Whether we share in some special experience or just sit and watch television, someone is certain to ask us: "How was it?" Our replies will range from "Oh, O.K." to "Hey, it was great!"

Have you ever thought what is behind such a reply? College students can be brutally frank. They can say of one course in the curriculum, "It's deadly!" and of another, "It's really exciting!" Behind the casual evaluations of our experiences lies the serious, though often unconscious, recognition that there is a vast difference between those experiences which enrich life and mere existence which brings death.

In his letter to the Romans, the Apostle Paul speaks of human nature in a bad sense. For him, life "in the flesh" is human nature dominated by sin and unable to save itself. Or as J. B. Phillips translated it: ". . . life on the level of the instincts . . . leads to certain spiritual death" (Romans 8:13).

Paul has given us this negative definition of human nature, and yet today's theologians say that we are "all being called to be human." Paul speaks of human nature as "deadly." Yet Ross Snyder, Harvey Cox, and other modern Christian writers view "human" not as deadly, but as a lively attribute.

What is it that makes the difference between human existence which is deadly and human experience which is alive and vital?

In Phillips' translation, Paul's words are: "But you are not carnal but spiritual if the Spirit of God finds a home within you." Paul is saying to you and to me: "You are not *dead* but *alive* if in fact God's spirit lives in you." "Come Alive" is the good news of Paul's letter.

The first dimension of Paul's imperative is: *Come alive — to God's gift of life that is in you.* The Spirit is the life force of the Body which is Christ and his members.

The possession of Christ's spirit makes us Christ's people. Do you know that this is what being a baptized Christian is all about? Baptism, for Paul, was actual participation by the believer in the death and resurrection of Jesus Christ. Buried in the water of baptism went the old, the "natural," man; rising up out of the baptismal waters came the new man, whose person became the home of the Spirit of Christ.

Paul asserts: "All who follow the leading of God's Spirit are God's own sons" (Romans 8:14, Phillips). He goes on to contrast *sons* and *slaves.* Slavery is fear; slaves are "up tight." Sonship is confidence and grateful joy. A woman had difficulty accepting herself. The fear that made her a slave was a sense of inadequacy. She was afraid that she couldn't do things the way other people would expect her to do them. For some time she had been part of an adult church school class whose members were encouraged to be part of the discussion. So one day she, too, spoke up. Her comment wasn't a long speech, but it was to the point, and other members of the class then built upon her contribution. No one knew at the time just how much that meant to her. Later in the week she called the pastor's wife and informed her that for the very first time in her long lifetime she had dared speak in public. Her acceptance by that class and by that teacher had allowed her to "come alive." She had been a slave of fear; now she was at liberty as a true child of the Father, God.

These strangleholds of fear are called "hang-ups" in the modern jargon. Saints are made when they are set free from their "hang-ups." From reading St. Augustine's *Confessions,* we become aware that he was a slave of sexual impulses. His "hang-up" of obsession with sex was removed from him one day. He began that day as a slave; he closed that day as a free man.

Martin Luther, as a monk, had a deep sense of his own inadequacy; he felt totally unworthy of his important responsibilities as a priest. So severe was this fear of his that he was actually a slave of his neurotic concern to be perfectly obedient. He was captive to his compulsion to be perfectly pure. Then, through studying the Bible, reading Paul's writings, and becoming acquainted with both Paul's and Augustine's delivery from such slavery to fear, Luther himself was set free. Once a slave, now a son.

"Free at last, free at last, thank God Almighty, I'm free at last." This spiritual, which grew out of a black people's terrible acquaintanceship with slavery, also communicates the joy that comes when we are no longer *slaves* in the fields of life but *sons* in the household of the father.

Discovering our intimate fellowship with God, we exclaim, "Abba! Father!" The words express an experience of intense awareness. This Aramaic word "Abba" was no doubt the first word in the Lord's Prayer. To say "Abba, my father" is to express self-recognition as a son in the circle of God's family. To know this relationship is to come alive to God's gift of life that is in each of us.

A young mother was having difficulty performing the day-in-day-out, monotonous responsibility of caring for her little children. She felt that living for her was an endless existence of washing up, feeding, bedding down, cleaning up. Then there was always a pile of clothes to wash, dry, sort, iron, and mend. Just when it appeared that her resented slavery would drive her to self-destruction, an older woman, who was a widow and member of the same congregation, came to her aid. At first the older woman just helped clean up, sort out, and straighten up the litter of the little ones. Then later, even days and weeks later, when it seemed that example and assistance were not enough, she resorted to words. Gently but firmly she said something like this: "Jean, don't be a slave to your emotions. You are free, Jean, free to enjoy your children, to watch them play and grow. Jean, trust in God. He helped me when I had as many children as you, and mine were fatherless. *Come alive, Jean, to the power that can work through you."* One Christian woman's faithful witness, first through deeds and then through identifying testimony, helped another woman discover the freedom that comes when God's love in Christ does set us free from our fears.

So the first thing we say is that "come alive" is a personal invitation to let the Spirit of God work within one's whole personality.

The second dimension of Paul's imperative is: *Come alive – to others.* The Apostle's words challenge us to open ourselves to others, even as the life principle of the Spirit can be seen in others.

Indeed, one can hardly come alive if he is set apart from others. Notice that Paul's letter is written to a congregation of Christians at Rome. Paul seems to take for granted that the gift of the Spirit does not come to individuals alone but that the Spirit is given to the expectant community.

The life in the Spirit is life in community with others. Indeed, alienation and estrangement from our fellowmen can be a form of death. Hostility is a form of slavery. Remember Jesus' words on reconciliation with one's brother: "If you are about to offer your gift to God at the altar and there you remember that your brother has something against you, leave your gift there in front of the altar and go at once to make peace with your brother. Then come back and offer your gift to God" (Matthew 5:23-24, TEV).

To come alive requires that we have living (that is, vital) relationships with our fellows.

Unfortunately, our times are marked by an increasing alienation between people. Quite visible are economic gaps between rich and poor, cultural gaps between black and white, gaps between political leadership and the voters, gaps between older and younger generations. If any gap becomes absolute separation and if gaps become total alienation and complete rupture, then our society is in danger of death. Intolerance is a symptom of alienation, a disease which leads to death.

For a person, for a family, for a society *to be alive* means to be open to other people, to all kinds of people. Openness toward others allows God's Spirit to move freely, breathing life into our relationships.

Two experiences will illustrate how men come alive to others. Some years ago several Baptist missionaries in Burma became friendly with some Roman Catholic missionaries. This contact began in days when estrangement rather than openness marked the relationships between Protestants and Catholics. Indeed, some of their early meetings in Burma took place in secrecy in order not to offend members of their respective communities. Then history caught up with these missionaries. When Vatican II opened up possibilities for closer cooperation among all Christians, one of the first pulpit exchanges anywhere in the world took place in Rangoon, Burma, when a Jesuit priest spoke in a Baptist pulpit. Who knew then that shortly thereafter all missionaries would be forced to leave that country? That act of reconciliation between Baptist Christians and Roman Catholic Christians left the Christian community of Burma with a life-enriching example of cooperation, an attribute which is essential today to the Christian churches in Buddhist Burma. The act of extending the hand of friendship to other Christians continued to be a vital witness to the faithful church long after both Protestant and Roman Catholic missionaries were forced to leave the land of Burma.

A further illustration of coming alive to others is from Linfield College at the time when students there became acutely aware of the black revolution. Several factors contributed to the Christian concern which developed. Baptist pastor Rev. Samuel McKinney, of Seattle, helped. A course in black history was initiated by Dr. Elmer Million. Convocation speakers addressed the regular weekly assemblies. The Christian Student Union conducted programs, and student dinner groups met weekly to discuss current issues. All these helped to develop a growing awareness that a Christian liberal arts college has a responsibility and opportunity to help provide higher education for some of our less advantaged fellow citizens. Student initiative, plus faculty support, plus the cooperation of the administration led to a student group called ACTION and a scholarship fund honoring the late Dr. Martin Luther King, Jr. Rather than students invading the administration offices with demands, the administration and students together helped plan, develop, and promote ACTION. As the first concrete result, thirty additional nonwhite students from all over America came to Linfield for the next school year. This group was in addition to the already significant international contingent, many of whom came from sister churches in Africa and Asia. Linfield College is coming alive because of the openness to others displayed in this recent history.

Thus, the invitation to enter into adventure with the Holy Spirit is not only an invitation to come alive as a person but also an invitation to come alive to others.

The imperatives of the Apostle Paul involve personal and social aspects of living, and his challenge also calls us: *Come alive — to God's gift in the world of men and of history.* He invited the individual Christian and the Christian community of his time to come alive to the action of the Holy Spirit in human history. The early church witnessed in turbulent times. The world was "a'changing." The people were restless, looking for a suitable philosophy that would provide some purpose to life. The people of that ancient world were looking for some moral and ethical standards by which to measure the meaning of life.

Now if members of the Christian church could come alive to the tremendous power of the Holy Spirit at work in them, in others, in all the world; then that church could change all the world. But first of all the Christians had to determine whether they would fear the changes — or change their fear into confident faith.

We live in a world very much like that ancient one. Old empires are fading; new nations and peoples are on the rise. Old authorities are passing away; new voices and new groups are demanding their place in the sun. Many who have enjoyed the substance and glory of the past are afraid of the changes which roll back the present and open up the future. Shall we Christians of today fear change? Or shall we change fears into faith? *The fear of change is slavery. The promise of faith is sonship.* Shall we come alive to the work of the Holy Spirit in history? "For you did not receive the spirit of slavery to fall back into fear, but you have received the spirit of sonship" (Romans 8:15, RSV).

There have been periods in history when Christian leaders feared change and fought it. When the printing press was invented, the first book printed was the Bible. But church leaders feared the change. Bibles had always been hand-lettered in monasteries. Bibles had always been in Latin, the language of the scholars. Church authorities were afraid of the change and refused to allow the printing of the Bible in the language of the people. The Reformation was the story of the people who were not afraid to change – people who had *come alive* to the possibilities of God's Word in the people's tongue.

Again, the English Christian authorities feared the spread of church authority from the hands of the bishops and presbyters into the hands of the congregations and the laity. They feared change, and they fought it. Men who were alive to the possibilities of change fled England and helped to found the United States of America.

Now what are the changes that the persons and classes in authority fear today? Do some fear sharing the responsibilities of power with blacks and browns? Do we fear allowing people different from us in tradition and temperament to share in the shaping of our national destiny? Why are we so afraid of the poor? Why are we so angered by the hippies? Why are we so confused by the audacity of Dr. Benjamin Spock and Yale's Chaplain William Sloane Coffin, who openly declare to the U.S. government that the conduct of the war in Vietnam is immoral? Are we afraid to face our cautious compromises?

Fear of change is bondage. Let us come alive to God's gift of life in history. When we walk in the Spirit, we are sure of liberty and life. The changes through which we are living can be occasions for confidence and grateful joy.

If we are alert to the very real possibility that God is working through the changes of our time to bring about his purpose for mankind, we can be set free to shout with joy when we see the divine rule of love, justice, and equity coming into being. We can speak with equal vigor wherever we see signs of the demonic forces which breed hatred, injustice, and inequality.

Knowing that God's Holy Spirit works through us, through our fellow human beings, and through human history, each one of us comes alive to the immense possibilities of human experience.

Come alive to God's gift of life in you – this is the personal invitation.

Come alive to God's gift of life in others – this is the social and community dimension.

Come alive to God's gift of life as evidenced in history – this is the human situation.

Come alive – for, in fact, it is God's Spirit who lives in you.

6
BECOMING AUTHENTIC PERSONS

Romans 12:1-13

So then, my brothers, because of God's many mercies to us, I make this appeal to you: Offer yourselves as a living sacrifice to God, dedicated to his service and pleasing to him. This is the true worship that you should offer. [2]Do not conform outwardly to the standards of this world, but let God transform you inwardly by a complete change of your mind. Then you will be able to know the will of God — what is good, and is pleasing to him, and is perfect.

[3] For because of God's gracious gift to me, I say to all of you: Do not think of yourselves more highly than you should. Instead, be modest in your thinking, and each one of you judge himself according to the amount of faith that God has given him. [4]We have many parts in the one body, and all these parts have different functions. [5]In the same way, though we are many, we are one body in union with Christ and we are all joined to each other as different parts of one body. [6]So we are to use our different gifts in accordance with the grace that God has given us. If our gift is to preach God's message, we must do it according to the faith that we have. [7]If it is to serve, we must serve. If it is to teach, we must teach. [8]If it is to encourage others, we must do so. Whoever shares what he has with others, must do it generously; whoever has authority, must work hard; whoever shows kindness to others, must do it cheerfully. (1-8)

The Apostle Paul had little use for religious practice or theological talk which was not transferable or translatable into human conduct and personal character. His letter to the Romans, for example, is one of the most theological documents in all of human literature. Here is a whole theology in a single letter, and right in the middle of it are practical recommendations on how to be an authentic human person.

Three practical suggestions drawn from Romans 12 can help in developing a sane estimate of ourselves, which will help us to become truly human.

Paul advises his friends: "Do not think of yourselves more highly than you should" (Romans 12:3, TEV). A friend of mine told of his own experience in this matter. He had just graduated with a master's degree in engineering from Michigan State. Discovering new goals for his life's work, he entered Yale Divinity School. One of his first assignments as a theological student was the leadership of a neighborhood youth group in one of New Haven's blighted areas. After he had spent a short time with the group, one small boy looked up into the face of my friend and very plainly said, "Don't take yourself so damned serious."

My friend listened to that urchin's advice and sought to "unlax," to slip out from under those prerogatives and pretenses that one so easily assumes. The little tough's straightforward criticism has helped my friend many times since.

But Paul, in saying, "Don't think more highly of yourselves than you should," was not simply saying something that any worldly-wise eight-year-old might tell us. Paul went on to say, "Each one of you judge himself according to the amount of faith that God has given him." You are what you are in relation to your Father God.

That advice explains how one can increasingly become the quality of person that God intends one to be. Paul was saying, at the very least, that the true setting for emerging human personality is not the lonely isolation of the wise man as pictured by the stoic philosophies of the Greeks. Rather, Christian personhood comes into being because of life within the Christian group, that church and that community which is the living body of Christ.

For real personality to emerge within the Christian community, the *humility* which Paul recommended is absolutely indispensable. Let's look more closely at this word "humility." I am afraid that the humble man in our time is caricatured as a "Casper Milquetoast." Humility in current terms is too easily connected with expressions like "coming hat in hand," or "just a doormat to be stepped on." I would like to try a different way of describing humility, which I see as an important Christian and a most human virtue: *Humility is accommodating our humanity in order to allow others to be more human.* In such a definition we find that humility means expressing our humanity in such a way that we encourage others to express their humanity.

I was so impressed with something that a missionary once said that I wrote it down. He said that he measured his ministry in these terms, that "the place where I am is becoming more of a human place to be."

Jesus seemed to have a similar standard for his own mission. Not one of us will deny that Jesus was human and that Jesus was humble. Yet Jesus was never a doormat, especially not for the Pharisees. He stood up to them, berated them, and called them names. "Whited sepulchre" is not exactly a term of endearment. Yet Jesus could accommodate his personality in order to allow the personhood of another to emerge. This is well illustrated in

Jesus' experience with the Syro-Phoenician woman who pleaded for help. Jesus at first responded as any good Palestinian Hebrew teacher would: "Let us feed the children first; it isn't right to take the children's food and throw it to the dogs." Then when she persisted, "Sir, even the dogs under the table eat the children's leftovers," Jesus came all the way around. He granted this Gentile woman the blessing she so badly wanted by healing her daughter. The humility of Jesus is shown in that he accommodated what he was in order that others might become more like what they were meant to be.

Paul's first recommendation for drawing up a sane estimate of one's personality was: Don't think of yourself more highly than you should. The second part of his advice clearly implied: Don't think any less of yourself than you are. Of course, those exact words are not found in Romans 12, but here is what Paul wrote: "Offer yourselves as a living sacrifice to God" (12:1, TEV). To understand fully what he meant, remember that Paul was one of the leading Pharisees. They were the very people who sought to fulfill all of the religious laws, including the laws which dealt with ritual sacrifice. As a Pharisee, Paul knew full well that only the very finest of the flock, only the best of the field's crop, was acceptable as sacrifice.

In Oregon, school children go into the strawberry fields to help the farmers harvest the crop. Any school child there can tell you whether the strawberries are from the newest (or first-year) planting or the older (second-year) planting. The first fruit of an Oregon strawberry crop will range from the size of a plum to that of a peach. The second year's crops are more like the smaller strawberries Easterners know.

Paul believed that only the very best of the crop was good enough for sacrifice, and he called every believer to present himself as a living sacrifice. Thus, "Do not think any less of yourselves than you are" is the very plain message.

The ritual of sacrifice was central in the Judaism of Paul's time. The temple in Jerusalem was still the center of the faith. The blood of the sacrificed animals was the symbol of the source of life. Paul wanted Christians to let their lives be the source of the divine energy, which was represented in the blood of sacrifice. Just as the divine force was present in the ritual of sacrifice, so the divine presence must be evident in the life and actions of Christ's followers.

Don't think any less of yourself than you are—you are worthy of presentation as a living sacrifice. But, we may plead, we are not spotless, we are not without blemish, we are not worthy of presentation before the Almighty. Paul recognized this when he warned: Don't think of yourself more highly than you should. But Paul also said in effect: "Judge yourself by the faith *God* has given you. You have been made spotless, your blemishes have been cleared up, you have been made into the first fruit of humanity by the love of Jesus Christ for you. Because Christ died for you, and because Christ *lives* in you, do not think any less of yourself than you are." Paul urges us to offer ourselves as living sacrifices to God, dedicated to his service.

Many years ago, there lived a shoemaker. His shop was probably like a one-man shoe repair shop we see in our smaller towns today. He had very little opportunity for education of the formal sort, not being of the social class whose sons went to the university. I don't think he ever gave much thought to improving his social status. But he was aware that his life was meant to be a living sacrifice. And so, as he bent over the leather and the shoe lathe, he concentrated on learning languages. This Englishman mastered Greek, Hebrew, Latin—tap, tap, tap—made shoes—mastered French, German—tap, tap, tap—made shoes—tap, tap, tap—this cobbler made history! William Carey's acute awareness that he was meant to be a living sacrifice unleashed the modern missionary movement. His lifework contributed to India's written language, science, and literature.

There is power in this affirmation: You are worthy of being a living sacrifice. I have heard Martin Luther King, Sr., and Lady Jackson (better known as Barbara Ward, British writer and economist) both state the same truth in different ways, but essentially this is it: When you tell any man that he is a child of God, and he believes you, then stand back, because you have planted the seeds of a revolution.

First, don't think of yourself more highly than you should; second, don't think any less of yourself than you are; and third, when you have made a sane estimate of yourself, *invest what you really are.*

Paul wrote: "So we are to use our different gifts in accordance with the grace God has given us" (Romans 12:6, TEV).

But, you may say, what have I to invest? I am only a housewife. I am only a teen-ager. I am only a retired person. I am only a student.

With the Apostle Paul, I say to you: *Invest yourself.*

Even though the problems are very big, let us not succumb to the paralysis of bigness which makes us seem impotent and powerless. Often people believe that the only solutions to *big* problems are *big* projects, *big* expenditures, and *big* ventures.

But some big problems can be solved by little means. Or better stated, the solution to many big problems will come when some little person invests all of his resources in bringing about a resolution of the problem.

For example, America has long had a growing, immense problem of the pollution of its countryside, its air, and its waterways. The problem has been apparent, but little was done about it because the nation has been paralyzed by the immensity of the task of cleansing its filthy environment. But one woman decided to do something about it. I remember sitting in the gallery of the United States Senate and hearing a number of senators eulogize Rachel Carson for awakening Americans and setting them free to do something about their environment.

We have long been aware that there are vast numbers of unemployed men and women who are jobless because they lacked skills. But one congregation in Philadelphia, under the leadership of Rev. Leon Sullivan, began a small program which grew and now is a model for a vast governmental effort.

America has a major crisis in mental health. Can the problem be solved by building vast, new hospitals? Certainly, adequate facilities for healing are needed. Some psychiatrists suggest that the best answer lies in a great many little people who care – friends, neighbors, Scout leaders, church school teachers.

Ross Snyder says that *caring* is feeling what is happening, being concerned about what can happen. Essentially, Snyder says, caring is loving; it is being *for* the other. Caring is "what man most fundamentally is."[1] "So we are to use our different gifts in accordance with the grace that God has given us" (Romans 12:6, TEV).

Don't think more highly of yourself than you should; but again, don't think less of yourself than you are. So, having made a sane estimate of who you are, become an authentic person, and invest all that you are. Invest in caring, to the glory of God and the service of your fellowman.

[1] Ross Snyder, *On Becoming Human* (Nashville: Abingdon Press, 1967), p. 135.

7

SENSITIVITY—A SIGN OF MATURITY

Ephesians 4:11-16

11 It was he who "gave gifts to men"; he appointed some to be apostles,
others to be prophets, others to be evangelists, others to be pastors and
teachers. 12 He did this to prepare all God's people for the work of Christian service, to build up the body of Christ. 13 And so we shall all come
together to that oneness in our faith and in our knowledge of the Son of
God; we shall become mature men, reaching to the very height of Christ's
full stature. 14 Then we shall no longer be children, carried by the waves,
and blown about by every shifting wind of the teaching of deceitful men,
who lead others to error by the tricks they invent. 15 Instead, by speaking
the truth in a spirit of love, we must grow up in every way to Christ, who
is the head. 16 Under his control all the different parts of the body fit together, and the whole body is held together by every joint with which it is
provided. So when each separate part works as it should, the whole body
grows and builds itself up through love.

How can we determine when a person is mature? We know that the number of years of age does not measure one's maturity. We sometimes say that a person is in his "second childhood." Others never seem to outgrow their first childhood. All of us recognize our need to grow up, as the letter to the Ephesians counsels: ". . . we shall no longer be children . . ." (Ephesians 4:14, TEV). However, neither can we forget the words of Jesus: "Whoever does not receive the Kingdom of God like a child will never enter it" (Luke 18:17, TEV). How can we reconcile the need to grow up and yet be like a child?

Jesus was talking about childlike characteristics. Paul, in Ephesians, was talking about childish characteristics. To be childlike is to have enthusiasm, express trust, live in honesty and open affection, and possess a keen sense of curiosity – to be sensitive to the world around us. The opposite of these virtues is childish behavior.

Have you noticed how selfish children can be? They demand, "I want that toy," and they wrestle for the one tricycle or the one doll, even though there are lots of other toys to be shared. *Selfishness* is childish, but adults are not immune to this ailment.

In its quarterly business meeting, a congregation, of which I was a member, voted to write to our senators and congressmen opposing the United States policy of seeking a military victory in Vietnam. I was taken to task by an older woman for this public stance. I tried to share with her some of the congregation's concern that innocent children and women were being murdered as our planes destroyed primitive Vietnamese villages. "Oh," she admitted, "there are innocents injured in every war." When I declared that, as a European veteran of World War II, I could not speak so easily of the death of others, her instant reply was: "Isn't it better that they die in Hanoi rather than San Francisco?"

Is it better that it is *their* women and *their* children who die? Or is such an argument a childish chauvinism, a cruel adult selfishness?

Another childish characteristic is a short attention span. Have you noticed how a toddler will start across a room toward some prized object, but halfway across his attention is attracted by something else, and he forgets his first goal and moves in a different direction altogether? Politicians and other mass-media persuaders seem to count on this childish quality among adults.

For the 1968 Democratic Convention, Chicago's Mayor Daley rushed a program of Potemkin villages. You may recall that Catherine of Russia's prime minister erected picturesque villages along the vacation routes of the Empress. These were like Hollywood film-set facades or false fronts behind which no actual villagers ever lived. In Chicago along the route of the delegates to the Democratic National Convention from their hotel to the stockyards convention center, Daley hastily erected prefabricated housing. The mayor counted on the short attention span of Americans to obscure the record that nothing had been done for eight years in these neighborhoods. Then, overnight, prefab houses went up.

The American public seems to have a terribly brief attention span. In a very short time we have witnessed the assassination of three of our greatest men – John F. Kennedy, Martin Luther King, Jr., and Robert F. Kennedy – but we forget so soon. One man who is not forgetting is America's first astronaut, John H. Glenn. He is vigorously pressing a campaign to register all firearms. He points out that we register to marry, to drive a car, to go to school, to vote, and to receive social security, and that none of these commonplace forms of registration abridges our freedom as citizens. Why, he asks, is there such reluctance to register a weapon of terrible destructive power?

Why, I ask, are we so prone to forget the tragic and repeated experience of death by assassination?

Lastly, our *adult childishness is marked by the limited point of view.* And I don't mean the lack of vantage point such as a small child experiences. "I can't see the man, Daddy," she says, and her father puts the child up on the counter so that she can see. Adults too often lack a place from which to see.

As adults, we are often guilty of having a limited point of view. For example, our middle-class prejudices are at work when we say: "Anybody can get a job if he really wants one." Are we aware that only the skilled are employable, that only the educated are sought after, that only the well-trained need apply in our technological society? To avoid childish opinions, we must grow in our awareness of the true facts of life.

To move beyond childishness requires growth. Paul says: ". . . grow up in every way . . ." (Ephesians 4:15, TEV). We need to grow in personal, family, and community relationships, socially, economically, and politically.

Growth, in many ways, is a natural thing. Is growing, then, doing what comes naturally? No, not entirely. For in nature, as any gardener will testify, weeds grow just as naturally as flowers.

So it is in human experience. Rousseau, the French philosopher, gained much of his fame by espousing a doctrine of allowing children to grow up close to nature, explore nature, and do without formal learning until late in life. Of course, what Rousseau wrote and what Rousseau practiced were two entirely different things. He fathered several bastard children, all of whom were placed in public orphanages far from nature's beauty, and none of whom, though they bore his name and parentage, were ever visited – even once – by their natural father.

Human growth takes more than what comes naturally. Growing as a process of becoming human involves not only natural development, but also expansion in responsibility.

Let's not allow this word "responsibility" to throw us. For

many of us, responsibility is a kind of burden, a sort of "ought" – "Since I am responsible, I ought to do this."

It may help if we see responsibility in terms of response. I exercise my responsibility to my loved ones as I respond to their humanness. I exercise my responsibility to my fellow workers as I respond to them as persons. I exercise my responsibility to my fellow citizens as I respond seriously to their human needs. In this sense, responsibility is closely related to sensitivity.

The human response to other human persons is a key that can turn responsibility from a burden into a shared privilege.

Many of us have administrative responsibilities. These can be burdensome unless we find ways to share them with others. This apportioning means more than passing out jobs or passing off tasks to others. For example, part of my college responsibilities include administrative duties in the student personnel area. As long as these duties are seen solely as responsibilities, the students are apt to be "its" – student blocs, student cliques, student power groups. But when I can see my responsibilities as responses, students become persons. How do I respond to Carol or to Larry? How can I most humanly respond to the student government or to the staff of the student paper? *Response* is the key, *relationship* the process, by which both students and student personnel administrators grow.

As you and I respond to others through our responsibilities, we can grow; others can help us to grow; and others can grow themselves. What directs our growth; how do we know we are growing?

In biology there is the factor in plant life known as "tropism." When children plant seeds in little plastic cups, nobody worries if the seed is planted right side up. (Bulbs are another matter.) Any person who grows African violets knows that the flowers grow toward the sunlight. This characteristic is tropism – the turning toward the source of life-giving energy.

Paul not only said to "no longer be children" and then to "grow up in every way," but he also tells us the direction in which we are supposed to be growing. He described the source of power that calls our humanness into growing reality.

". . . We must grow up in every way to Christ, who is the head. Under his control all the different parts of the body fit together . . ." (Ephesians 4:15-16, TEV). Just as the sun is there drawing the seed out of the dark ground into the light, just as the sunshine draws the emerging flower and leaf in its direction, so the love of Jesus Christ draws human personality into being.

Note carefully that the Apostle Paul here spoke of our corporate growth. We as a Christian community are being drawn under Christ's control until all our different personalities, our many different gifts and experiences, our own unique contributions become like different parts of the body, fitting together to be effectively the body of Christ. Paul was not interested in this discussion of the body of Christ in order to increase theological jargon. The experience of community was real for him. And the same experience is terribly – or wonderfully – real for us, depending on whether we lack or possess such Christian community.

I have a growing conviction that great congregations help develop great Christians. The corollary is also true. Weak and flabby congregations help to produce weak and flabby Christians.

What separates the weak congregations from the strong ones? Not size – for there are big but weak congregations, and there are small but strong congregations. Not location – for there are plenty of weak congregations in suburbs (where congregations are supposed to flourish), and there are a few strong congregations in the inner city (where we have assumed that success can't happen).

Then, it must be a grasp of the right theology which enables us to produce better Christians. While there is some truth to this assumption, all of us are aware that neither conservative theology nor liberal theology is the most important factor in developing spiritually able-bodied Christians. I can name strong and effective congregations with a liberal theology, and I can name strong congregations with conservative theology; but the factor which helps these dissimilar congregations to develop vigorous and fruitful Christian personalities is that Christ is acknowledged as the genuine head of a living body. The direction of the Christian fellowship is provided not alone by a strong leader, or a strong theological stance, or a strong denominational loyalty, or a strong power structure, or a strong church program. The effective Christian congregation develops when the believing fellowship lives its corporate life with a conscious recognition that Jesus Christ is the head, calling the authentic community into being.

We are in danger of slipping away into theological abstractions unless we recognize that Christ's authority measures the values that guide our family life; that mercy and justice as visible in Christ are the measures of how we invest ourselves in our community; that humanity and equality as demonstrated in Jesus Christ are the fair measure of the loyalty we owe to our nation in relation to the loyalty we owe to all mankind.

Thus, we are challenged to grow up, to become mature. Let us outgrow our childish behavior, our childish chauvinism, our short attention span, and our limited points of view. Let us grow in the most responsible way possible, that of sensitive response in fully human relationships. Let us grow together into that fullness of humanity which is possible when together we grow into the stature of Christ.

8

OUT OF THE CRUCIBLE

1 Peter 3:13-17; 4:12-16

[13]Who will harm you if you are eager to do what is good? [14]But even if you should suffer for doing what is right, how happy you are! Do not be afraid of men, and do not worry. [15]But have reverence for Christ in your hearts, and make him your Lord. Be ready at all times to answer anyone who asks you to explain the hope you have in you. [16]But do it with gentleness and respect. Keep your conscience clear, so that when you are insulted, those who speak evil of your good conduct as followers of Christ may be made ashamed of what they say. [17]For it is better to suffer for doing good, if this should be God's will, than for doing wrong. (3:13-17)

Much of life seems to be a matter of stumbling along — until we stumble into a place of decision making. We try to do our best, but often enough our best misfires. Then we are in an even worse human predicament — until we are thrown into a test. Moses was stumbling along, filling in as a shepherd until he stumbled upon the burning bush — his test — and a people were set free. The German priest Martin Luther was sort of stumbling along, in that form of academic stumbling peculiar to professorial types, until he stumblingly posted ninety-five theses in the Latin jargon of the scholars. Somebody put his paper into the people's German, and the Reformation was on — Luther had come into his time of testing.

Rosa Parks literally was stumbling along. Weary on her feet, she took a seat on a Birmingham bus. Now a time of testing came for Rosa Parks, for the people of Montgomery, Alabama, for all Americans — and the new American revolution was under way.

So we stumble through life — until our time of testing comes when we are thrust into the crucible.

The word "test" comes from the Latin "testa," which is the word for the earthen vessel used in the earliest prescientific experimentation to test for true and basic physical elements.

The early Christians lived constantly under the threat of severe persecution. What lessons for today can be gleaned from the terrifying experiences of those early Christians? From Peter's letter I would draw three major areas for our consideration. First, the presence of the Christian community in the world *tests the world;* second, the presence of the Christian community in the world *tests the Christian church;* third, the presence of the Christian community in the world *tests God.*

Let's begin with the first assertion: The presence of Christians in the world tests the world. The letter known as First Peter states: "Who will harm you if you are eager to do what is good?" Then the letter writer, immediately recognizing the real situation, writes, "But even if you should suffer for doing what is right, how happy you are!" (1 Peter 3:13, 14, TEV).

By its very existence, the authentic Christian faith is in contention with every other ideology that would strive for the faith of men. Today Christian people are called to stand in the midst of an anxious age and demonstrate that their confidence does not lie in the intense search for security; to stand in an acquisitive society and show clearly that more things do not create a true culture; to stand in an aggressive society and illustrate plainly that certainty does not lie in mere acquisition of power.

The conscientious Christian cannot conform to the existing patterns and ideologies. When he asserts, "Life is more than this," he is contesting what is.

The Christian faith says "nay" to a scientism which would turn humans into objects to be manipulated according to the mechanical determinism of self-styled rational men who have elevated scientism to a modern religion.

The Christian faith, by its very presence, says "nay" to a nationalism that would require blind and dumb allegiance to whatever a nation does in its own sovereign interests. True Christian patriots stand forth for eternal ideals which transcend the party rationalizations and justifications of those who would place the national state in that ultimate position of authority which belongs solely to God.

The Christian faith says "nay" to a racism which would reduce human flesh to pigmentation and would measure a man by the way his epidermal layers reflect the waves of light. Truly Christian men have professed the unity of the human race and have invested their lives in the cause of brotherhood. The world has tried to silence such witness, but the blood of the martyrs cries out to our own generation.

The Christian witness tests this world of ours – and the world wishes that Christians were silent, or would go away, or would continue to stay irrelevant. Thus the world says: "Stay out of this, preacher, it ain't the business of the church. Don't meddle – stick to your praying and preaching."

The Christian presence tests a world which emphasizes power – military power, economic power, political power. In a power-inflamed world the Christian often stands powerless – powerless in that meekness in which he believes that the world is his to inherit.

In today's world where man is convinced that nothing matters but the "right now," the Christian presence witnesses to a living connection with the saints of the past, the living spirit in the present, and a living hope in a future.

In a world that wrestles to control whatever it can get its hand on to control, the Christian presence affirms that all of time and existence – past, present, and future, is under the control of God.

The authentic Christian presence is a judgment on the presumptions of the world in which we live. But the tragedy of our day is that this Christian presence is barely distinguishable. It is so hard to tell the Christian man from the non-Christian. Consequently, quite often the judgment upon our world comes from the most worldly of sources.

Hollis Alpert, commenting in the *Saturday Review* on the film *The Graduate,* indicates that the author of the original script, Charles Webb, deliberately intended to write an immoral satire on an immoral society. So immoral is the film that it has become perhaps the most moral film of our times. Its judgment upon our social practices is illustrated in one scene where the graduate, just home with a degree from an Eastern establishment university, is being toasted at a cocktail party honoring his achievement. A friend of the family puts his arm around the graduate and in an awesome whisper promises to give him the key word to success. Later, the time to tell comes. The graduate and the entire audience wait for the word to be revealed. What is the word that will save all of mankind?

What is the word that will change the course of history? The graduate leans forward and listens. "Plastics. There is a great future in plastics."[1] In the theater the teen-age audience howls – and the middle-age audience cringes, for this is the moment of truth for all of us. I myself felt torn. The man of the mature years in me identified with the middle-aged patrons in the movie theater. Certainly plastics is a good business investment. But the other part of me, that which has sympathized and identified with college students for so many years, screamed loudest: "What a phony world! Look what plastic has done to our world; everything is plastic and everything is fake. We're in danger of being buried alive in the litter of plastic being dumped upon us!"

If the Christian presence should fail to bring judgment upon our world as it is, then God will use the immoral voices of the world to state the moral judgments our times deserve.

The Christian presence *tests* the world, and the Christian presence in the world also *tests* the Christian church. The faith expressed in First Peter reminds us of Jesus' words: "Do not be afraid of those who kill the body but cannot afterward do anything worse" (Luke 12:4, TEV).

Recently a Japanese graduate student asked an American high school student, "What are your life plans?" "I'm thinking about sociology," replied the American. The Japanese student, half jokingly, half seriously, asked, "Sometimes sociologists are accused of being Communists. Aren't you afraid of that?" "Oh, no, those are just words," said the high schooler. But will the Christian congregation of which that young person is a part support this insight, or will the high school student be forced to give up his idealism because the congregation temporizes with the existing folkways of the community around it?

[1] Hollis Alpert, *Saturday Review*, July 6, 1968, pp. 14-15, 32.

Will the church fear the social forces of the times, or will the fear of God drive out all other fears?

While spending some days in the southern United States recently, I became acquainted with a controversy under way in the Presbyterian Church, U.S., which is the Southern Presbyterian Church.

The debate began with the June, 1968, issue of their official magazine, *Presbyterian Survey*. The editors "asked a panel of Negro Presbyterian pastors to help plan this special issue, to say, kindly if possible, belligerently if necessary, what the white Christian must know in order to deal with white racism, which is, after all, the cause of the crisis." [2] The special issue was entitled "Love Shall Overcome." The cover showed the mule cart bearing the coffin of the Christian martyr, Martin Luther King, Jr. The lead article was excerpts from Dr. King's famous epistle, "Letter from Birmingham City Jail." In the August issue of the magazine the editors printed some of the letters which they had received. Several accused Martin Luther King of being a subversive. One correspondent wrote: "You have to expend money and energy glorifying Martin Luther King, Jr., who is and was responsible for more deaths than Al Capone. I am sure you are aware of his Communist connections. . . ." Here is an excerpt from another letter: ". . . I have one child, which is a nine year old daughter, and there are a number of magazines which I do not approve of her reading, but including *Playboy* the *Presbyterian Survey* would be at the bottom of the list. I do not pretend to know the Scriptures well enough to debate with you at that level; however, I have my conscience which has been unchanged in this line of thinking for some time. I do not believe you all can make this statement. . . ." [3]

There were also letters in support of the editor, calling the special issue "excellent." But I share these critical comments with you, not because they reflect on Southern Presbyterians, but because they reflect on all of white, Christian America. The

[2] *Presbyterian Survey*, June, 1968, p. 3.

[3] *Presbyterian Survey*, August, 1968, p. 6. Copyright August, 1968, *Presbyterian Survey*. Reprinted with permission.

Christian church is being tested by this issue of racism. Have we the love, the fortitude, and the conviction to address the demon which lurks within the breast of American society and command, "In the name of God, I demand that you come out."

In that same August issue of the *Presbyterian Survey* there is evidence of yet another way the Christian community is being tested. The Southern Presbyterians had just completed their General Assembly. The pages who served on the floor of the General Assembly were drawn from their seminaries. At the close of the assembly, the pages wrote a general letter which said, in part:

> We leave thankful at having met and heard many such [Christian] people; but more than that, we leave with huge question marks glaring in our minds: Why were important ethical demands smothered by a superficial quest for denominational face saving? Why was there such a lack of decisiveness on the part of commissioners? Why were we unable to feel a genuine spirit of love and sincerity? Why did the responses made to the poor, the unloved, the discriminated against, seem unreal and phony? [4]

Then the seminarians signed their names. They were the student-body presidents and outstanding students of the denomination's own seminaries. We must confess that the leading seminary students in every denomination would probably say the same things about their congregations and official conventions.

The presence of the Christian in the world *tests* the world; the presence of the Christian in the world *tests* the Christian church.

Lastly, the presence of the Christian in the world *tests* the power of God. Our presence in the world tests whether our relationship with God is a live connection or a broken connection. Any of you who have watched an electronic repairman fuss over a speaker-cable can sense the real difference between a live wire and a broken, dead connection.

Man, in a sense, is in contention with God. In the Broadway musical *Fiddler on the Roof*, the Polish Jew, Tevye, in a few soliloquies has a word with the Almighty. In the rich tradition of a certain kind of Jewish piety, the man contends with his

[4] *Ibid.*, p. 18.

Creator. At first the argument is at a very human and very humorous level. Tevye wonders why God has "blessed" him with five daughters? But later the altercation becomes a real one when the Jewish peasant demands to know of God why the constables are allowed to beat and maim the Jews in a vicious pogrom.

One is reminded of the exchange between Job and his Creator in the Old Testament. Calling the Eternal to task, Job himself is sternly asked, in effect, "Who are you? Why, you are hardly capable of holding up your own pants." The stern address from the Almighty to mortal man: "Gird up your loins . . ." (Job 38:3, RSV) is also the saving word, "Stand like a man."

As we stumble through life, testing and being tested, we come upon the ultimate test: We demand of God that he demonstrate his presence and his power. Our demands are met by cosmic counterdemands, "Gird up your loins," and the conferral of dignity, "Stand like a man."

Stumbling – tested – standing in full human dignity, we, like Jacob, may walk with a limp for the rest of our lives; but we have wrestled with the Almighty, and we know the blessing that can come only from him (see Genesis 32:22-32).

We began by noting that the word "test" came from *testa*, the earthen vessels used in the earliest scientific experiments. In God's plan he has a small earthen vessel he is using for his experimentation. That earthen vessel is man. You and I in our stumbling come to the testing. As we wrestle with poverty and welfare cases, Vietnam and politics, racial crises and neighborhood causes, may our wrestling, our contending, our testing in the crucible lead to God's blessing. Through *testing* we are becoming human.

9

FROM CONFRONTATION TO FREEDOM

1 John 1:5-2:5*a*

5 Now this is the message that we have heard from his Son and announce
to you: God is light and there is no darkness at all in him. 6 If, then, we say
that we have fellowship with him, yet at the same time live in the darkness,
we are lying both in our words and in our actions. 7 But if we live in the
light—just as he is in the light – then we have fellowship with one another,
and the blood of Jesus, his Son, makes us clean from every sin.
8 If we say that we have no sin, we deceive ourselves and there is no
truth in us. 9 But if we confess our sins to God, we can trust him, for he
does what is right – he will forgive us our sins and make us clean from all
our wrongdoing. 10 If we say that we have not sinned, we make a liar out
of God, and his word is not in us. (1:5-10)

When students feel that the administrative officers of their college have overlooked some important factors in reaching a decision, they demand a confrontation. They want to brush aside the thicket of the bureaucracy and come face to face with the persons who actually make decisions. Today's students believe this procedure is the only way to begin to work out a solution, the only way they can be truly free to find answers to their problems. In a much more profound way, if we are to be free to become truly human, we must first of all confront the God whom we worship.

The kind of human persons you and I are becoming depends on the God whom you and I worship. If we worship an austere and remote deity, our product is either a remote and austere personality—or a rejection of such a God and such a style of life. The deities we worship provide the pattern for human personality and the structure for human society.

The writer of the First Letter of John was well aware of this phenomenon. The verses which we will examine in this passage have to do with the God the writer of this letter has known and experienced.

". . . God is light and there is no darkness at all in him" (1 John 1:5, TEV). The letter of James says that God ". . . does not change, nor does he cause darkness by turning" (James 1:17, TEV). Note the emphasis upon the constancy of God. God as portrayed here is not whimsical and moody. When people first read this letter, they recognized that the one described here was not one of the Grecian gods.

Those early Christians lived in the Roman world, which had adopted the religion and the gods of ancient Greece. About all that the Romans did to naturalize the gods was to give them Roman names. Those of you who have read the ancient writer Homer will recognize the marks of primitive Greek religion. The gods were just a little more than mortals. They inhabited Mount Olympus, from which they would swoop down through the towns and villages of the mortals whenever boredom or meanness dictated. The gods were licentious and often took advantage of the beautiful girls and the handsome young men. Why did these ancient gods act as they did? They had no apparent reason. They did whatever they felt like doing. In short, the Olympian gods were capricious, immoral, and untrustworthy. On the human level, blind fate seemed to shower a person with more possessions than he could ever use in one day, and then they would be taken away another day.

So bad were the reputations of these gods that first the Greek poets, then the playwrights, and later the philosophers emerged to wrestle with the human questions unanswered and unresolved by the Olympian religion. One poet, Euripides, dared to say: "If the gods do aught that is base, then they are not gods." [1]

The God of the Bible was different from the gods known to the Greco-Roman World. Where the gods of Mount Olympus were whimsical, the God of Mount Sinai was trustworthy. Where the god Zeus and his kin were tyrants, the God of Israel was just. Where Zeus and the Olympian deities were immoral, the God who disclosed himself to Abraham and Moses was compassionate. "Jahweh," the name by which God identified himself to Moses (Exodus 3:14-15, RSV), heard the cries of the captive people in Egypt and wanted them to go free. Jahweh saw the pitiable plight of orphans and children in Amos' day and sent the prophet to set down a plumbline of justice. The God of

[1] J. Calvin Keene, et al, *The Western Heritage of Faith and Reason* (New York: Harper & Row, Publishers, Inc., 1963), p. 241.

Abraham, Isaac, Jacob, and Jesus sees what modern men and societies are doing in what we grandly call Aid to Dependent Children. The God who cares for his children is the God of the Hebrews. The One who works for justice is the God revealed in history. The God who has compassion for humankind is the God we see in Jesus Christ.

"God is light and there is no darkness at all in him," states the Scripture. He is not fickle; he is not devious; he does not equivocate; he does not temporize. God is straight, just, merciful, compassionate. We can believe, with Ross Snyder, that as humans we are basically created to find life rather than death, fullness rather than emptiness. We say this because life and meaning are what we see when we turn to God as disclosed in Jesus.

So the first word from this letter of John is "light up" by turning your face toward God and seeing him as he is. In his light you can discover what your humanness is intended to become.

Then, the second word is "face yourself." See yourself as you really are. Let God's light help you to see and "tell it the way it is."

If honor and honesty are marks of God as revealed in Christ, then in all honesty we must confess who we really are. "If we say that we have no sin, we deceive ourselves and there is no truth in us. But if we confess our sins to God, we can trust him, for he does what is right – he will forgive our sins and make us clean from all our wrongdoing" (1 John 1:8-9, TEV).

The fact that we can count on God to be just and constant in his response allows us to act and behave in a way that encourages our human growth. Here we come to the subject of *confession.* Why is my confessing what I really am, what I have really done, and what I really think, essential to my becoming human today?

Perhaps there is nothing which holds up and holds back our personal and social human development as much as our pretensions. We tend to pretend to be other than we are. We pretend so much and so often that in a little while we forget who we really are. If we live long enough in such a half-real, half-pretend world, we will end up as sick personalities.

But it hurts to be honest about myself. Do I really have to level – do I really have to own up to who and what I really am? And with that question, we are smack in the middle of the whole human drama. We can recognize scenes from Shakespeare, a scene from *A Streetcar Named Desire,* and a scene from our own life.

Can I really face myself the way I really am? There's a terrible price to pay to be honest about myself – can I afford it?

This Scripture encourages us to face toward the light that radiates from God's compassionate face. Trusting in him, we are enabled to come clean, to confess who we really are, and to become increasingly human because we are increasingly honest about ourselves.

In the present era in human history, Christians are called to grapple with the social dilemmas of the times. One of the confessions which we are called to make is the acknowledgment of the sins of our fathers, and we must confess further that we have often benefited because our fathers sinned. In England today some of the landlords and the nobles have to close down their vast estates because they cannot afford the servants needed to keep up the countless rooms and hundreds of acres. Those estates were built in the past out of the sweat of colonials and the hard labor of Englishmen in the mills and industries, and now enlightened Englishmen can no longer exploit their own fellowmen nor do they have the colonies to exploit. Economists refuse to state this awful truth boldly. If they say it at all, they say it in academic jargon hidden behind a defense line of scholarly footnotes.

Or allow me to say it in personal terms. Since both my father and mother migrated to the United States in the last days of the Hapsburg monarchy, I could alibi that the racial crisis was a problem that was here long before their coming. But I was born in these United States, and I was born white; those two facts indict me. I am a beneficiary of the white establishment; and I am, in some measure at least, responsible for the policy which has systematically excluded blacks and browns from sharing in the full benefits of the American way of life. What is my responsibility when I read a news article about the bombing of a Negro church? Can I pretend that I am *not* responsible?

As a Christian, the gospel makes it possible for me to be honest about those social structures which have benefited me and which now stand under judgment. "If we confess our sins to God, we can trust him, for he does what is right. . . ." I am confident that God's promise holds true for the sins which I share corporately with others as well as for those sins for which I personally am responsible. And I can be honest about my personal hates, browbeating, and indifference toward my fellows and my loved ones for the same reason I can confess my complicity in social and corporate sins: Because God does not cause darkness by turning, God will not turn his back on you or on me.

Whenever I come to wrestle with the Scriptures and our present-day situation, I am filled with the sense of awe that overcame Isaiah: "Woe is me! For I am lost; for I am a man of unclean lips, and I dwell in the midst of a people of unclean lips . . ." (Isaiah 6:5, RSV). Brethren, "if we confess our sins to God, we can trust him, for he does what is right – he will forgive us our sins and make us clean from all our wrongdoing."

When we confront God as just and realize that we have to be set right with him, and when we honestly confess the real character of our human situation, we are open to wonderfully new possibilities for our humanity.

"But if we live in the light – just as he is in the light – then we have fellowship with one another . . ." (1 John 1:7, TEV). Because God is honest, and because we, by confession, are honest with ourselves about ourselves, we are set free to have honest-to-goodness relationships with our fellows.

Some time ago I came to know Louis Mitchell, a preacher and a sociologist. I owe to Lou what I call "Lou's Lexicon." He added a number of words to my language. One of these is "bag." When I first heard Lou say that, my mental image was of those polyethylene bags in which suits and dresses come back from the dry cleaners. After these covers caused a few deaths by suffocation, warnings were printed on the plastic bags. I wish there were ways we could put warnings on certain "bags" which will suffocate us if we get enclosed in them. The bag of white man's culture can smother us to death. The bag of middle-class morality smothers – a morality that we preach about in public and on Sundays but that we fail to practice as we sneak out of town or away to a businessman's convention. A newsman cynically noted the flood of prostitutes into the city where a political convention was being held while the delegates were publicly making strong platform pronouncements about law and order in the streets. That bag of a double-standard morality is certain to smother any person, any society. And if we are really interested in finding out what are our double standards, we can ask any honest hippie. But we should be prepared to listen for quite a while.

How do we get out of these bags which are certain death? The First Letter of John not only says that God is trustworthy and that we need to confess, but it also promises if we are honest with God, he'll help us.

Altogether too many of us have been brought up on a religion of "oughts": you ought to do this – you *ought* to behave like that. I find myself every day betraying this moralistic perversion of the gospel, for the actual Good News is: I am free – free to enjoy all of life with its ambiguities and complexities – free to enjoy all kinds of people – free to involve myself in all the kinds of enterprises, projects, and programs which are intended to assure legal and social freedoms for others.

What does it mean to be free? It means that I no longer have to prove myself; I can give freely of myself in the best direction I know of, the best way I know how, and I can count on God to make use of whatever success or failure comes of my effort.

Being free, which means really counting on God, saves us from being spoiled by success or made desperate by failure. We are free because we trust in God, who can be trusted, and because we have been honest about ourselves. This kind of freedom enabled Martin Luther King, Jr., to stand upon the mountain and look out with confidence upon the promised land; for he had found who he really was, and he knew a God on whom he could really count.

10

BRIDGING THE GENERATION GAP

2 Samuel 15–18; Ephesians 6:1-4

Children, it is your Christian duty to obey your parents, for this is the
right thing to do. 2"Honor your father and mother" is the first command-
ment that has a promise added: 3"so that all may be well with you, and you
may live a long time in the land."
4Parents, do not treat your children in such a way as to make them angry.
Instead, raise them with Christian discipline and instruction. (6:1-4)

In every age since woman first gave birth to a child, young persons and their elders have had difficulty understanding each other. The problem has become so intense in our time that we even have a name for it — the generation gap. The problem is certainly more complex than it ever has been before. Only in a few other periods of rapid social, economic, and historical change have young persons and older persons experienced the extensive difficulties of communication we now encounter.

Today we are experiencing more than the usual parent-and-child estrangement that in some measure must mark any maturing process. Today the various generations do see their world differently. This difference in understanding and perception aggravates the differences between the generations.

Assuming that a very real generation gap does exist, are there ways that we can bridge the chasm between generations? If we are to span the generation gap, *we must first be ready to recognize the differences* between our generations.

Each generation experiences a different childhood, a different adolescence, and a different early adulthood than the previous generation because of the two decades that separate parent and child. However, what is so significant today is the radical difference between the childhood of the parent and the childhood of the child. For example, in the course of a recent conversation a man asked, "You remember Amos 'n' Andy, don't you?" Yes,

I do, and I remember Tom Mix, Jack Armstrong, and hot summer afternoons broken by the sounds of neighbors tuned in to hear the baseball games. Television was something I didn't expect to see until the twenty-first century. Certainly, we had motion pictures, but we had to go to a theater to see them. Remember the newsreels? If the news was less than five days old, we thought we were witnessing a scoop. In contrast, today children view the latest happenings from Vietnam or the Middle East while they munch on their TV dinners. What Marshall McLuhan has made plain is something any mother might have told us, if we had thought to ask. Our children today are visually oriented. They see things in moving imagery, in black and white or living color. Life now comes in picture-tube size. Batman is more real than Daddy's boss. Captain Kangaroo is more of a moral influence than Billy Graham or the Pope – except, perhaps, when the evangelist or Pope Paul appear on the television screen.

Another way in which the generation gap is manifest is the alienation that exists between veterans of World War II and those who have come of age since then. This alienation is possibly the most severe in all of American history. Much of our government's foreign policy is based on some form of anti-Communism. While this policy seems to make sense to older citizens who have been preoccupied with the cold war for more than twenty years, to the young such a policy often seems out of date and even irrelevant. Young persons seem to have little difficulty in choosing between coexistence and coextinction.

We may very well be experiencing the kind of serious breakdown of communication between generations that led to the American and Russian revolutions. A gap between generations can become just that serious. However, my intention is not simply to create fright, but to call attention to the need to identify what is different between our generation and that of our children and of our children's children.

The biblical King David might have saved himself a great deal of heartache, and his nation a good deal of internal strife, if he had seriously thought through the differences between his generation and that of his sons. The Second Book of Samuel in the Old Testament might be called the Book of David. Here we find a chronicle of this very great, this very human, personage – David the King. His son Absalom wanted to seize power. Absalom gathered such a following that the king was forced to unleash his military might to destroy the rebellion. In the fighting, Absalom was killed. As we read this fascinating chronicle, we might well ask, "Was this rebellion necessary? What might David have done to prevent the discontent? How might he have allowed his son to invest his energies in pursuit of useful and attainable goals?" My own opinion places the responsibility as much on David as upon his son. He allowed things to drift until the only course of action remaining was to unleash military power. In effect, this policy not only destroyed his son but also a large part of the nation. In turning back his beloved son and his loyal supporters, David was destroying the best of what he had spent his whole life bringing into being.

When the generation gap widens into open hostility between generations, the inevitable result is the severe damage of both the senior and the younger generations. There is ample evidence in both the Bible and in all history that the generations may destroy each other if the generation gap is not bridged.

When we have recognized what is different between generations, we need to go on to find *what we have in common with other generations.*

Each generation has a beginning, and each has a destiny. Birth and death are common to all generations. The long process of life – beginning with total dependence upon others, then continuing in growth of body, mind, and self-identity, the developing of increasing self-dependence, the assuming of responsibility, reaching out and making one's own circle of friends, taking on a job and career, beginning one's own family, being part of life's joys and sorrows, glorifying in victories, braving defeats – this process is common to all. The life process in its fundamental aspects is unaltered for every human generation. What is different for each generation is the attitude which that particular generation brings to the process.

We hear a great deal about the present young generation being a "now" generation which seems to ignore the past and is agnostic about the future. This young generation is interested in the "happening." Let it be concrete; let it be vivid; let it be *now!* As one seventeen-year-old put it: "Our generation isn't sure there's going to be a tomorrow – even though we keep running into it. We have to have yesterday, today, and tomorrow all at once." His remarks fairly summarize a widely held and even more widely publicized attitude today.

The older generation needs to listen attentively and sensitively to this word that comes from the younger generation. The generation over thirty years of age needs to take those under thirty more seriously. At the same time, the younger generation needs to take itself less seriously. For its own survival, the "now" generation needs to look more closely at the reality of the life process in which it finds itself.

I have noticed that the sensitive young person is able to break out of his peer-group isolation when there are young children or old folks around. Naturally the average young person has a keen sense of curiosity. To remember what it was like to be a child and to wonder what it is like to be old are natural questions. Curiosity leads the self to break out of its "ego-ghetto." One's interests are enlarged by tuning in on the interests of others quite different in age. One student told me how he broke with some avant-garde "way-out" personalities when these supposedly liberated individuals acted unkindly and with needless cruelty toward an innocent child. Whereupon, the student thought, "Why, they're not liberated people at all. They're just selfish slobs."

Nature abhors the "now" when the present is isolated from what has been and what is yet to be. All generations share in the process of life, which has a common beginning and a predictable close.

The "now" generation stands to lose the potentiality of humanity – the what-can-be, which is hidden in the simplest child. How did Jesus describe the great potentiality of God's coming rule?

When Jesus defined the requirements for entry into God's kingdom, and again, when he proposed to his disciples a model of what it means to be great, he turned to a child. In childhood we can observe directness, humility, the dependence upon love; we can see trust rendered without the calculation of gain. We also find in children an uncanny shrewdness in detecting deceit. We notice, too, that they have a natural way of refusing to be closed in by the routine social customs.

In short, all generations — the young, the older-younger, the younger-older, the old — can learn by reflecting on the similar beginnings and the similar endings to this wonderfully varied process we call life.

Thus far I have suggested as steps toward the bridging of the very real generation gap that first we recognize in what ways we are different, and second that we recognize what we have in common. Finally, we can bridge the generation gap as *we recognize that we need one another.* That no generation is an island unto itself is the meaning I find in Paul's words:

> Children, it is your Christian duty to obey your parents, for this is the right thing to do. "Honor your father and mother" is the first commandment that has a promise added: "so that all may be well with you, and you may live a long time in the land."
>
> Parents, do not treat your children in such a way as to make them angry. Instead, raise them with Christian discipline and instruction (Ephesians 6:1-4, TEV).

Paul saw a mutual relationship between children and parents. As generations, we do need each other. No generation is truly independent. Wisdom recognizes the need and interdependence of all generations.

Allow me to share a personal experience to illustrate this. I know a pastor in a large church who regularly went to the seminaries to call young men to serve their first charge after graduation as associate ministers of that church. He did this regularly, in part to keep from growing old and to keep from getting out of touch with change. This openness towards youth characterized not only the pastor but also that congregation. And what of the young men who came to serve that congregation? They also learned to be open to all ages. They worked with children, youth, adults, and persons in the leisure years of life. Accepted as responsible leaders without regard to their youthful age, they in turn were set free to accept all persons without regard to age.

I find in the Christian gospel that each of us is to be free to be himself. In the perspective of the gospel, age is just another of the dividing walls of hostility that has been pulled down. The generation gap has been bridged by the One who will always, through all time, stand astride the dividing line so arbitrarily set by today's "now" generation. Jesus stands astride the thirty-year mark. He is the angry young man who was executed for the crime of upsetting the status quo. He is also the One who spoke of the worth of early years and the glory of the closing years. And Jesus admonished his disciples: "Let the children come to me! Do not stop them, because the Kingdom of God belongs to such as these. Remember this! Whoever does not receive the Kingdom of God like a child will never enter it" (Mark 10:14-15, TEV). Although Jesus lived very much in the now, he did not forsake the future. "'Do not be worried and upset,' Jesus told them. 'Believe in God, and believe also in me. There are many rooms in my Father's house, and I am going to prepare a place for you'" (John 14:1-2, TEV).

Recognizing that each generation stands in need of the generation before it and the generation that follows, are there some practical ways of building bridges between the generations? Here are a few suggestions, none too spectacular but all of proven value. The element common to all these suggestions is the sharing of various meaningful experiences. I recall, for example, when my wife's father came to visit us, he would try to see that I went with him to see a baseball game. During the last such visit, three generations of men enjoyed a game at the ball park together. I know of a mother who regularly makes a habit of taking her daughter on a shopping trip. Family vacations are another way of either bridging or deepening the gap between generations, depending on what use is made of the time together.

An important method of bridge building is conversation that

includes a wide-ranging variety of interests. The table talk of Christian families can be a way of bridge-building while at the same time widening one's world view. Two senators and a president of the United States came from around that family table where Joseph Kennedy talked world politics and Rose Kennedy taught simple Catholic piety. Children can be encouraged to bring current events to the family table. The family's opportunity for conversation can be increased where families learn to play games together – table tennis, badminton, or any of a number of table games. Whatever the mutually shared interest, people of different ages and skills can gather around something of a common concern. One family I know has bridged a considerable age gap because they all share an enthusiastic concern in civil rights and peace. Their motto seems to be: The family that demonstrates together stays together!

Such dialogue across age lines is important. Lloyd Averill has written:

> Too rarely do young people have opportunity for . . . meaningful relationships with adults. . . . As a result, the adolescent peer group takes on the function of forming the young person's image of what it is to be an adult. That this image is frequently distorted and unreal, and that in desiring to be thought of as an adult the adolescent will claim freedoms and choose forms of behavior that are really caricatures of adult life, should scarcely surprise us.[1]

This statement applies to more than the teen years. All of us, whatever the age, need to recognize the possibility that we can be trapped into living in the world of only those of one's own age. While it is important for personal development that a person be able to identify with his own age and interest group, it is equally important that he not limit himself completely to those just like himself, in age or in interest. For us to limit our circle to others just like us is to succumb to the tyranny of the peer group. We obey the most cruel tyrant in all history when we do something because that is what "they" are doing.

[1] Lloyd Averill, *A Strategy for the Protestant College* (Philadelphia: The Westminster Press, 1966), p. 86. Copyright © 1966, W. L. Jenkins. Used by permission.

Even though the current generation gap is greater than the normal estrangement between parent and child (so much so that it is a chasm divides our culture and makes a cleavage that tears through the social fabric) we need not give way to despair. Although there are real differences between the various generations, all generations have in common life itself in its full sweep from birth, childhood, youth, adulthood, leisure years, and finally, to death. This process of life places upon all generations a situation of mutual need. Because we all stand in life, we stand in need of one another.

All of us are caught up in the interrelationships of life, including the problem of the generation gap. My life is that of a son to a father — one generation — and a father to a son — another generation. Yet I am confident that this serious issue yields also to the influence of the Christian gospel. King David's unfortunate experience with his son may be our experience. However, the thoughtful parent will reflect on King David's experience, the Apostle Paul's instruction, and our own modern-day situation. The act of reflection can be followed by decisive living, as we are secure in the faith that the love of God the Father has overcome the chasm that gaps between the divine and human. Jesus Christ is that One who enables us to be about the process of bridge building.

11

LIVING LIFE'S SECOND CHOICES

Luke 14:7-24

15One of the men sitting at the table heard this and said to Jesus, "How
happy are those who will sit at the table in the Kingdom of God!" 16Jesus
said to him: "There was a man who was giving a great feast, to which he
invited many people. 17At the time for the feast he sent his servant to tell
his guests, 'Come, everything is ready!' 18But they all began, one after another, to make excuses. The first one told the servant, 'I bought a field, and
have to go and look at it; please accept my apologies.' 19Another one said,
'I bought five pairs of oxen and am on my way to try them out; please
accept my apologies.' 20Another one said, 'I have just gotten married, and
for this reason I cannot come.' 21The servant went back and told all this
to his master. The master of the house was furious and said to his servant,
'Hurry out to the streets and alleys of the town, and bring back the poor,
the crippled, the blind, and the lame.' 22Soon the servant said, 'Your order
has been carried out, sir, but there is room for more.' 23So the master said
to the servant, 'Go out to the country roads and lanes, and make people
come in, so that my house will be full. . . .'" (15-23)

Having guests for Sunday dinner seems to be an ancient custom. Luke records an occasion when Jesus attended a dinner that was quite a social affair. In fact, the anxious, status-conscious behavior of some of the guests drew a comment from Jesus. His remarks about humility prompted another dinner guest to exclaim piously, "How happy are those who will sit at the table in the Kingdom of God!" (Luke 14:15, TEV).

In reply, Jesus told the parable of the great banquet (Luke 14:16-24). The emphasis of Jesus' story is on the refusal of the guests who were first invited. The story can be examined from another perspective also, that of the guests who were invited only after the first-choice guests had refused to come. Let us focus on these persons who lived out life's second choices, the persons who were chosen last of all. Careful study of the parable may illumine our own experiences. When we face life realistically, we find out that we must live out our second choices. To speak of living life's second choices is to speak with stark realism, for life often does press us to accept something less than our first choice.

As human beings we constantly deal with and must live with second choices. We may go to the college of our second choice or take the job and enter the profession of our second choice. We would choose to live out life in graceful long years with a beloved companion, and yet we may be called to live a somewhat lonely second choice. Each of us desires good health, yet many of us are called to live a second choice with a heart disease or some other physical limitation. These second choices carry with them much greater significance than the minor preferences of life, such as the desire to own the latest model automobile or the decision dictated by necessity to hang on to the old model. Such temporary and insignificant setbacks are not real disasters, for nothing of great importance is changed by them. We are not concerned in this discussion with life's minor reversals and petty disappointments, irritating as many of these may prove to be. Rather, our attention is upon the real second choices that permanently affect the total course of an individual's personal destiny and a community's corporate development.

In the parable, Jesus sensitively portrays men and women who are living out life's second choices. He speaks of the poor, the lame, the crippled, and the blind. These people are the very ones who are unlikely ever to be able to pay back any kindly benefactors. In our own times persons still live with these limitations. In our generation we have seen men and women demonstrate the heights of human dignity that can be attained by persons who will live out life's second choices.

One such person was Anne Frank, a young Jewish girl, who lived in Amsterdam during the German occupation of the Netherlands. For two years she lived hidden with seven other persons in a small and secret cluster of rooms in back of her father's former place of business. Her diary tells of the life of two families living in constant danger of discovery by the Nazi troopers. Thus, Anne Frank recorded the thoughts of a young girl living under extraordinary conditions. For over twenty-four months of her adolescent years, she was enclosed in the small compartments located above some storage rooms. Yet her sensitive spirit overcame these narrow limits. Anne Frank may have wished often for the first choice of a normal teen-ager's life: to ride a bicycle in the streets, to go to school, to play table tennis, and to enjoy some ice cream afterward. But with life's second choice she constructed a world to which she gave some hope and meaning, even despite its apparent hopelessness and meaninglessness. Wherever free men gather to describe nobility and courage, Anne Frank will be remembered, for she lived out life's second choice and proved what it is to be truly human.

If the first characteristic we noted is that *life's second choices are real,* we must next recognize that *life's second choices cost something.* There is a price to be paid whether our experience is one in which we must accept our own second choices, or, in a different kind of experience, we ourselves prove to be the second choice of others.

Fifth grade in the public schools is as good a place as any other to begin to think about life. One young fellow was worrying about one of the other boys in his classroom. He expressed his concern in these words, "Charlie is always the last one to be picked for a team." Whether it is in picking sides for a softball game, or in being selected for advancement within the corporation, one of the most difficult human experiences is to be passed over. The clever designers of television commercials are very much aware of this human dread of being passed by, but to overcome our distress will take a great deal more than brand Boop-Boop in mouthwash, toothpaste, or deodorant.

The loss of one's first choice costs something. To have one's first choice denied or to be bypassed often brings hurt, pain, and anguish. Even to choose to accept the second choice costs something.

In Jesus' own personal history we can see how he faced the problem of making choices. His first choice seems to have been to bring about the reform of the Jewish church and nation from within the existing structures. In the earlier chapters of the first three Gospels, we note the urgent appeals which he addressed to the Pharisees, who were the acknowledged moral and spiritual leaders of the nation. When this first choice was denied and renewal among the religious leaders proved to be an impossibility, then Jesus was forced to the hard decision of living out his second choice. He decided to go to Jerusalem. He shared with his disciples his own anticipation regarding the high costs of this venture. We know that his forebodings were confirmed in tragedy.

The Garden of Gethsemane demonstrates the high cost that often goes with the second choice. Here the first choice of Jesus was evident in his prayer: "Father, if you will, take this cup away from me." His second choice was also apparent: "Not my will, however, but your will be done" (Luke 22:42, TEV). Jesus was confronted with the cost of the second choice. Men in modern times also face this awful cost.

Although the period of Adolf Hitler and the Nazi regime must appear very much like past history to today's young moderns, it is very much a part of our own era. Thus, those among us who want to understand the psychology of modern man turn to the work of a man like Dr. Viktor Frankl, the well-known Viennese psychiatrist. His careful study of the human psyche was put to the most cruel test in the death camp of Auschwitz. Viktor Frankl's first choice would have been to remain in the Austria of the days before Hitler, where his way of life was centered in his medical practice, his circle of friends, and the intimacy of his family. All of these associations were harshly denied him because he was a Jew. The members of his family were brutally separated from each other, and each began a lonely and horrible march toward execution. What does a man do in response to this final denial of all that has dignity and is human? Dr. Frankl survived for a long time in the bestial conditions of the concentration camps. There he found himself stripped down to a minimal existence. Gordon Allport described Viktor Frankl's situation: "His father, mother, brother, and his wife died in camps or were sent to the gas ovens, so that, excepting for his sister, his entire family perished in these camps. How could he – every possession lost, every value destroyed, suffering from hunger, cold and brutality; hourly expecting extermination – how could he find life worth preserving?" [1]

The hope-filled testimony of Viktor Frankl, out of his own desperate experience, is recorded in his book, *Man's Search for Meaning*. He writes, "Everything can be taken from a man but one thing: the last of the human freedoms – to choose one's

[1] Viktor Frankl, *Man's Search for Meaning* (Boston: Beacon Press, 1967), p. ix.

attitude in any given set of circumstances, to choose one's own way."[2]

Having been made aware that second choices are a real part of life and that such choices bear a high price, where can we find the strength to face the high cost of real second choices?

The Christian faith responds to the real and costly choices of life by affirming that man can live life's second choices with confidence. *Christianity attests to the faith of those who are the second chosen.*

As Christians, we are aware that we are not God's first chosen. This honor belongs to the Jews. This fact is reflected in the encounter of Jesus with the Canaanite woman (Matthew 15: 21-28). Jesus consistently said that his primary mission was to call the Jews back to God.

Remember how the Apostle Paul, in the letter to the Christians in Rome, reminded the Jews, not once but three times, that God's promise came to the Jew first and then to the Greek (Romans 1:16; 2:9-10). The Christians were not God's first chosen, and neither were they the first choice among their fellowmen. The Christians were those who, by and large, had been bypassed on the first go-around of the world's honors and favors. Again, the Apostle Paul reminded the Christians in Corinth: ". . . Few of you were wise, or powerful, or of high social status, from the human point of view" (1 Corinthians 1:26, TEV).

The early church probably found it easy to identify with the guests who were second choice in the parable of the great banquet, because these early churchmen were those for whom the Servant Christ had ventured into the highways and byways of life. They had experienced the surprise of the invitation and had come to join in the bountiful and festive supper. The First Letter of Peter described the early Christians this way: "Once you were no people but now you are God's people; once you had not received mercy but now you have received mercy" (1 Peter 2:10, RSV).

A Christian's faith sustains him because it is not built upon

[2] *Ibid.*, p. 65.

any lofty pretense but rather upon the sober recognition that although he had been passed over, God, in his gracious love, has taken the rejected and made him his own.

The parable of the great banquet demonstrates why those of the Christian faith can face with confidence the reality and the cost of life's second choices, for the parable tells of God's judgment and God's mercy. In the parable of the great supper the judgment is a warning of what happens when men betray their divine commission. God had entrusted a mission to the Jews; but, beguiled by the power and riches of the world, they refused their mission. Therefore, God turned to the "godless" and the "alien," even though these had been maimed by the cruelty of others and their own sin. In relating this parable to the church today, George Buttrick observes: "If the church becomes comfortable and self-righteous, God will gather in some secular movement that is lowly and contrite, baptize it with his own forgiving grace, and use it for his glad purpose." [3]

Even so, perhaps for those of us who are confronted with living out life's second choices, the promise of mercy stands out in Jesus' parable. In the comments which precede this parable and in the parable itself, Jesus mentioned the poor, the crippled, the lame, and the blind. These are the persons who must live out life at its second best. Particularly to such as these, Jesus addressed the good news of God's love. To those of us who are confronted by life's second choices, those who are poor in spirit as well as in body, those lamed by society's injustices as well as by physical infirmities, and those blinded by hatreds and bitterness as well as those whose physical sight is gone – to all of us, the gospel comes as good news.

This good news proclaims that God, too, has faced second choices, that God has lived out life's second choices in Christ Jesus, that life's second choices can be lived out in the victorious action of God's continuing love for each of us.

[3] George A. Buttrick, ed., *Interpreter's Bible* (Nashville: Abingdon Press, 1952), vol. 8, p. 256.

12

POVERTY IN THE MIDST OF PLENTY

Philippians 4:4-9

[4]May you always be joyful in your life in the Lord. I say it again: rejoice!
[5]Show a gentle attitude toward all. The Lord is coming soon. [6]Don't
worry about anything, but in all your prayers ask God for what you need,
always asking him with a thankful heart. [7]And God's peace, which is far
beyond human understanding, will keep your hearts and minds safe, in
Christ Jesus.
[8]In conclusion, my brothers, fill your minds with those things that are
good and deserve praise: things that are true, noble, right, pure, lovely,
and honorable. [9]Put into practice what you learned and received from me,
both from my words and from my deeds. And the God who gives us peace
will be with you.

A certain boy was beginning his first year in the public schools. Because he came from a wealthy family, his mother was greatly concerned that he not parade his wealth before his classmates lest they not accept him as one of them. So she spent some time coaching him. Her final words to him as he left for school were, "Now, don't you say anything about how rich we are."

The very first day in school every child was asked to write an essay about himself. So the little boy wrote: "My personal essay. I am poor. My mother is poor. My father is poor. Our cook is poor. Our upstairs maid is poor. Our gardener is poor. My lifeguard at my private swimming pool is poor."

Even though the comprehension that some of us have of poverty is hardly more profound than that of the little boy, poverty today is a rightful concern for all of us. There is poverty in our great and beautiful land, a great deal of it. A friend who is a professor of sociology at a theological seminary has expressed his fear that long after we have resolved the racial problem, we shall still have a more serious problem to solve, that of the great gulf which exists between social and economic classes within our society. We do need to cry out against poverty because it is wrong for poverty to exist in the midst of plenty.

Nevertheless, there is another form of poverty that stalks our land. It is a poverty which strikes the affluent as well as the destitute, which exists among the rich as well as among the poor.

Let me illustrate what I mean by sharing something that was said to a group of us who were visiting the Russian embassy in Washington. For the first time in my life I was standing on Russian soil, and I met a real, live Communist. The students who were with me asked him, "How do you like living in America?" His smile and the fact that he was smoking a pack of an American brand of cigarettes supplied the answer. When they asked him about his first impressions of the country, he replied that he was simply astounded by the large number of automobiles that he had seen. Then he added that although the people in Russia had nothing at all like our consumer goods – cars, clothes, appliances – he was also struck by how serious, how worried, and how anxious Americans appeared. He claimed that Russians had fewer goods, but they seemed to be happier. Even though Americans had far more automobiles, televisions, and other things, they seemed to him to be less happy. We can recognize the propaganda in the Communist's remarks, but we also must admit an element of truth in what he said. We are rich in the things of this world; but we are poor in the things of the spirit.

Now is the time to declare a war on the poverty of spirit that exists in our land today. If we are to mount an attack, we need to set forth the principles, or weapons, with which we will wage our assault on poverty. There are three major weapons on which I would rely in the struggle. These are three principles or ideas that can undergird any Christian person as he rids his own life of spiritual poverty. The same three principles can guide any Christian community, be it a local congregation or a whole denomination, as it bears down in the effort to root out spiritual impoverishment in society. Simply put, the three principal ideas relate to man, God, and Christ.

The first essential is man. If we are to overcome spiritual poverty, we must give man his proper place. We must recognize the *universality of man,* that every man is a unique person. As a specific illustration, think of the headlines which have come from the Vietnam war screaming, "486 Viet Cong dead." This same brutalization is practiced every holiday weekend when the auto fatalities are listed like a catch of fish. These dead are not statistics — whether the dead are the enemy or our neighbors killed on the highway. These are men — fathers to be missed by their children, husbands to be mourned by their widows, boyfriends to be missed forever by their sweethearts, and sons never to be replaced by their aging mothers.

If we are to be spiritually abundant, we need to include every man in our circle of concern. The only way I know how to include every man is to think of a particular man. If I think of alcoholics in general, for example, I find it too easy to dismiss the problem. But when I think of a particular alcoholic whom I have known, I think of the tragedy of an education wasted, a career ended, a family broken, and children left homeless and fatherless. Then alcoholism is no longer just another social problem but an enemy I have met in combat.

Thus I do not think of adultery as a general subject, but I think of a certain man who ruined his personality, destroyed his family, and created chaos in the lives of his children because of the act of infidelity and adultery. Nor do I discuss drug addiction as a general classification, but I think of a specific young man who ruined his life; he was literally burned out at twenty-five because of his turning to the use of drugs.

This principle of the universality of man simply means that, if we are to declare war on spiritual poverty, we need to name all men as brothers, and we need to know particular brothers by name.

The second of my three planks in a platform for a war on spiritual poverty is the knowledge that *God is presently active in history.* Our times are rapidly changing times. All about us we sense and often see upheaval. Yet in just this kind of world, I find God at work. There have always been acts of injustice as well as acts of justice in the world. I see God's hand in the acts of justice. The Jews who are described in the Old Testament helped us to look for God in his acts in history. The great act for the Jews in history was the Exodus from Egypt. Jesus himself observed Passover, which celebrates God's act of deliverance from Egypt; and the Jewish community today still remembers the act of God in liberating his people. But a part of that chapter in human history is the act of Moses in anger killing an Egyptian overseer. That was an act of injustice. The injustice of Moses or the injustice of the Jewish people who berated their leader for bringing them into the wilderness where they faced the threat of starvation should not obscure God's actions for justice in the Exodus experience. The injustices of our times should not blind us to the movements for justice in our times, movements in which I discern the powerful hand of God.

Let me try to illustrate from recent history. The first time that many Americans ever heard of Vietnam was through the writings of a Roman Catholic medical doctor, Thomas Dooley. Both the Vietnamese and Americans have reason to praise Dooley's ministry of healing. I would hope that long after the conflict in Vietnam, the healing and teaching ministry of men like Thomas Dooley will continue to be the mark of American interest abroad. I would prefer to have people in other lands know America through her medical assistance, her technical aid, and her agricultural specialists than through tanks, troops, or even tourists. It may be a small thing, but I see the reconciling work of God in the vast amounts of money being spent in agricultural and educational research now under way at many American universities; many of the results of this research will be used in other nations.

The missionary movement with its rural specialists, medical stations, and schoolteachers paved the way now being followed by governments. How ironical it is that many people today fail to find any sense of God's actions in and through the churches, rather they look for signs of God's action in other places.

If we are aware of all men as our fellows, and of God as an active agent in the history of our time, then we are well along in our preparation for this engagement to eradicate spiritual poverty. But we still need to find the power that can bring spiritual health. Since a handful of men first listened to and followed that humble teacher from Galilee, men and women have come to know that they find power to know God and relate to their fellowman through Jesus, whom we confess to be the Christ. Thus, the third weapon for our war on spiritual poverty is *faith in Jesus Christ.*

I am certain that many share what I felt when the young Communist in the Russian embassy said, "You Americans look so unhappy." We must admit that we do worry a lot and sit with long faces altogether too often. I know that I must confess I belong to the poverty class in spiritual matters. What is it that can set us apart from the Communist and give us a sense of confidence?

The young Communist may be just as concerned for his fellowman as I am, even if for different reasons. And, although that young Communist denies that God is at work in history, he does see a dialectical principle at work in history.

On those two counts, I rank fairly even with the Communist. But on a third count, I am both more free and more dependent than the young Communist. I am more free because I am dependent on Jesus Christ. The Russian embassy official's Communism may be like a religion for him. He has certain beliefs, or slogans, by which he lives. But my Christian life is not a religion — a set of rules, a certain list of obligations. My Christian life is a faith. I live in relationship to my fellowman and to God through my daily experience with Jesus Christ.

Jesus Christ makes it possible to "sit loose" to all the pressures of life around me. Being in Christ is the only justification I need. I don't need to prove how manly I am. I can be free to be a man because Christ has set me free. I don't have to prove anything to anyone, myself or the other fellow. Knowing that Jesus Christ has accepted me, I can accept myself; and thus I am freed from the anxieties of being found acceptable in my work, in my community, or elsewhere.

Christ makes it possible for me to "sit loose." I can do my best and yet not expect perfection, for Christ has already accepted me, imperfect as I am. Strangely enough, such an attitude often allows me to do far more than when I got myself all tied up trying to achieve perfection. In the midst of life's struggles come Christ's words to be what we are. We are invited to share in a style of life fitting for a Christian. This style seems almost casual, but it is tough and rugged, equipping us to fulfill God's purposes.

Let me illustrate from real life. Some time ago a man whom we call a great man was in prison. His life was daily in danger. There were all kinds of political maneuvers to get rid of him. He might well have wondered why he ever left his well-to-do family in the suburbs. Or he may have asked himself why he hadn't stayed at the university where he probably could have had a teaching post. But he did not worry about himself. Can you catch even a whiff of dungeon and danger in these words of his in a letter to some old friends?

> May you always be joyful in your life in the Lord. I say it again: rejoice!
>
> Show a gentle attitude toward all. The Lord is coming soon. Don't worry about anything, but in all your prayers ask God for what you need, always asking him with a thankful heart. And God's peace, which is far beyond human understanding, will keep your hearts and minds safe, in Christ Jesus.
>
> In conclusion, my brothers, fill your minds with *those things that are good and deserve praise: things that are true, noble, right, pure, lovely, and honorable.* Put into practice what you learned and received from me, both from my words and from my deeds. And the God who gives us peace will be with you (Philippians 4:4-9, TEV, italics added).

This man's attitude is truly an example of a Christian style of life. As such a style begins to catch on among us, we will move forward in our efforts to get rid of spiritual poverty in the midst of material plenty.

13

WHEN NOW IS NOT ENOUGH

Matthew 25:1-13

"On that day the Kingdom of heaven will be like ten girls who took their
oil lamps and went out to meet the bridegroom. 2Five of them were foolish,
and the other five were wise. 3The foolish ones took their lamps but did
not take any extra oil with them, 4while the wise ones took containers full of
oil with their lamps. 5The bridegroom was late in coming, so the girls began to nod and fall asleep.

6"It was already midnight when the cry rang out, 'Here is the bridegroom! Come and meet him!' 7The ten girls woke up and trimmed their
lamps. 8Then the foolish ones said to the wise ones, 'Let us have some of
your oil, because our lamps are going out.' 9'No, indeed,' the wise ones answered back, 'there is not enough for you and us. Go to the store and buy
some for yourselves.' 10So the foolish girls went off to buy some oil, and
while they were gone the bridegroom arrived. The five girls who were
ready went in with him to the wedding feast, and the door was closed.

11"Later the other girls arrived. 'Sir, sir! Let us in!' they cried. 12'But I
really don't know you,' the bridegroom answered." 13And Jesus concluded,
"Watch out, then, because you do not know the day or hour."

We are living in the time of the NOW generation. Although it had a legitimate enough beginning in the demands for "Freedom Now!" the movement has been taken over in part by the hippies who just want their kicks now. The emphasis is on the present moment. Live now. Enjoy now. Get it right now.

In a sense, there is nothing radically new in this attitude. Was it not the prodigal son who went to his father and said?—"Father, give me now my share of the property" (Luke 15:12, TEV). But the emphasis upon *now* is not limited to those who are in their late adolescent years. In some measure most of us are part of this *now* generation. Although older than the *now* generation, we are infected with a similar philosophy. We borrow now and repay later. We buy now and pay later. We fly now and pay later. The pleasures are now. The payments are deferred.

Certainly, we need to live each day, even every moment, to its fullest. However, every moment has its past, its present, and its future. Jesus told the story of a wedding celebration (Matthew 25:1-13). When the bridegroom came to the feast, everyone was invited to celebrate with him. However, there were some who had failed to make sufficient preparation. As they did not have oil for their lamps, they could not share in the moment of festivity. During the hours of waiting, they had given no thought to the future; as a consequence they could only look back with sorrow and remorse at what might have been. Although not denying the importance of *now*, we need to look ahead to the future and remember the meaning of our past.

My first major proposition is that all of us need to listen to the voices of the *now* generation. They may have something to say which we need to hear. In trying to put all of life's possibilities into what happens now, are they saying anything to those of us who have had more time to explore and experiment with life?

A teen-ager was explaining to her mother the latest version of the game of "chicken." Two young men on their motorcycles ride directly toward each other along the center line of the highway. The first to swerve out of the path of the other is "chicken." Obviously the risks of such a juvenile game run high with serious injury or even death as a possible consequence. When the mother asked, "Why do they do it?" the daughter commented, "Maybe they don't want to grow up, ever."

Although we can recognize that some adolescents are afraid of the responsibilities of adult life, could the reason be that we who are adults have presented an undesirable image of life? Do these young people reject the picture that we present of the rat race, the dog-eat-dog world, the frantic pursuit of the almighty dollar – or the almighty research grant, or the almighty publication?

Each of us, if he takes the stance of the *now* generation seriously, needs to inquire of himself: "Has my frenetic life betrayed those who look to me for an example of what it means to be an adult? What have I exhibited as I pursued life? Is the way I live a style of life that commends itself to others as being effectively and satisfactorily human? If I were twenty years younger or forty years younger, could I take encouragement from the way in which I live today?"

We must hear what those of the *now* generation say. If, by their own frantic efforts to contain the whole of existence in the present moment, they are, in effect, saying: "We reject the kind of future represented in what you have become," then they are passing a serious judgment upon our own styles of life.

We also need to recall that the passage of time has different values at different ages. For instance, in our town we have been discussing the establishment of a youth center. We have talked about it for at least two years. One boy reminded his father that at this rate the youth center discussions had little relevance for him: "After all, Dad, you're only a senior high student for three years." Those of us living in our creative years (some youngsters refer to it as old age) need to recall that time passes differently for different ages. Only the mature see patience as a virtue.

Thus, the *now* generation needs to be heard because it remind us of the importance of the present. Too many of us are caught up in what we are going to do someday. Or we are tied down by memories of the past. We have become so entangled in the past or the future that we ignore the wondrous possibilities of the present. We keep on planning for the docking of our dream ship, or we replay what we once did on some day long past. Thus, we may miss the grand opportunity of doing something right here and right now. The *now* generation may just help us wake up to all that is possible in the present.

You may recall the winsome scene from Thornton Wilder's play *Our Town* in the third act. Emily has died, and she requests that she be allowed to relive one day of her life. The stage manager agrees to let her relive her twelfth birthday. But the experience is too much; she can bear only a few minutes of it. As she settles into her new existence beyond the grave, she takes one more look. You may recall her words: "Goodbye! Goodbye, world! Goodbye, Grover's Corners – Mama and Papa – Goodbye to clocks ticking – and my butternut tree – and Mama's sunflowers – and food and coffee – and new-ironed dresses and hot baths – and sleeping and waking up! Oh, earth, you're too wonderful for anyone to realize you! (Thinking a moment, she half-turns to the Stage Manager, questioning more gently) Do any human beings ever realize life while they live it? – every, every minute?" [1]

Jesus himself emphasized the now. Very often he used such words as "now is the time." In Nazareth he stated: "This passage of scripture has come true today . . ." (Luke 4:21, TEV). To

[1] Thornton Wilder, *Our Town* (New York: Coward-McCann, Inc., 1939), act 3, p. 83. Copyright 1938, 1957 by Thornton Wilder. Reprinted by permission of Harper & Row, Publishers.

Zacchaeus he declared: "Salvation has come to this house today . . ." (Luke 19:9, TEV). Such instances of Jesus' emphasis on the present are numerous. Among his last words on the cross were the words of promise: ". . . today you will be in Paradise with me" (Luke 23:43, TEV).

If any single thing characterized the message and ministry of Jesus, it was his declaration that God's reign had broken into human life right here and now.

So we are indebted to the *now* generation for forcing us to reexamine how we spend our present moments. We are reminded of the wonder of life and the many varied possibilities for living in the present moment.

However, because we have recognized some values in the *now* generation, this recognition does not mean that we should accept the whole position of the *now* generation without further examination. In emphasizing the now, does one exclude both future and past from the present? Have some advocates of the *now* generation confused posturing with positive action? By attempting to force the situation *now*, have they confused activity with significant action?

Certainly the actions of some of the members of the *now* generation cannot be explained in any other way than that these youth hold a naive assumption that doing something right away is in itself an accomplishment. One fundamental weakness in the platform of the *now* generation is the failure to recognize that many important actions take place only if we plan and prepare for such action well in advance.

This brings us to my second major proposition. For the *now* to be significant, it must be drawn forth by the future. An important test question for any movement is: "What are your long-range expectations?"

Modern man has been so successful in mastering nature that some people have forgotten the urgency of planning. A young friend of mine walked over a pass in the Swiss Alps dressed only in his leather shorts. When he descended to the village on the other side, the native villagers couldn't believe anyone would be dressed so improvidently. When they told him of the sudden snowstorms which often closed the pass, even in summer, he was shocked by his own stupidity. He was particularly thankful for his good fortune thus far when the pass was closed by a sudden storm the next day.

I have traveled in parts of the Dakotas and Montana in what for easterners is late summer. There the automobiles of the wise plainsmen were equipped for bitter cold and heavy snows. Such preparedness can mean the difference between life and death.

Now the future which draws the present into being may be just a prudential concern. We plan ahead in order to survive. But the future of which I speak has more than just survival in view, for the kind of future that we anticipate gives birth to the tomorrows which we experience.

A favorite question which adults often ask children is: "What are you going to be when you grow up?" If we could only retain the wisdom of our childhood! Children tend to answer, if they answer at all, in terms of persons. "I want to be a daddy; I want to be a teacher; I want to be a nurse." They quite often express it in terms of persons who have helped them. Of course, by the time they get to college the categories are different. The service aspect is often less apparent. You can almost hear the sophomore saying, "I want to be $12,000 a year," or "I want to be status," or "I want to be success."

What do you want to be? What do you want the world to become? *Now* is not enough if it lacks the important dimension of the future.

In the Summer, 1967, issue of the *American Scholar*, Joseph Wood Krutch has written: "Can anyone deny that for at least a hundred years we have been prejudiced in favor of every theory, including economic determinism, mechanistic behaviorism and relativism, that reduces the stature of man until he ceases to be man at all . . . ?"[2]

I would go on to say that the stature of man is increased or diminished according to the dreams, goals, and visions of the future by which he allows his life to be shaped. With what kinds

[2] Joseph Wood Krutch, "If You Don't Mind My Saying So," *American Scholar*, Summer, 1967, p. 357.

of lifelong goals and with what kinds of dreams are we preparing for the future?

Many of Jesus' teachings emphasized this dimension of the future which determines how our present moments develop. A wedding was one of the greatest of all festivities in a Palestinian village. So important was it that bride, groom, and all the guests were free from their religious duties. The scholar could forsake his books, for his attendance at a wedding was a more important duty and privilege.

The custom of the bridesmaids to await the arrival of the groom seems to have been an accepted one. So Jesus used the practice as a parable of preparedness. The wise girls prepared in advance for the experience, but the foolish girls did not think ahead and thus they had no reserve of oil for their lamps.

There are many experiences in life when nobody else can go in our place. Either we have prepared ourselves, or we are unprepared. The *now* generation ignores the fact that Martin Luther King, Jr., had prepared himself through college, seminary, and doctoral studies for the moment of history that came in Montgomery, Alabama. There are certain things that cannot be obtained at the last minute. There are certain things in life that cannot be borrowed. These we must win or possess for ourselves. We cannot borrow them from others.

The Christian Good News derives its power in the present because it centers on the hope out there ahead of us. We must not ignore the many fundamentals of the faith which deal with the future. The second coming, the final judgment, the resurrection of the dead, Christ's Lordship over time and history — all remind us that the dimension of the future is essential to the Christian faith. Remember the Lord's Prayer, "Thy kingdom come, thy will be done." These elements are all part of the Christian faith. A vision of the future is essential to life in the present.

We need to think carefully about the future hope because it gives meaning and direction to the present. *Now,* by itself, is not enough. The future which we strive for today will make the "now-moments" of tomorrow either a dream or a nightmare.

We must see the future as clearly as did the grandfather of a friend of mine. The man knew at the time he planted an oak tree that he would not live long enough to enjoy its shade. The children of his sons would be the ones to play and grow under the tree. But he planted well, and there grew up a beautiful tree. The children of that family went out to the mission field. On each furlough when they returned, they rested under the oak tree and thought of the future dreamed of by a grandfather who dared to invest in his posterity.

Just as that great tree spoke to the present of the hope of the future and the dreams of the past, so our *now* needs to be guided by the hope of the future and by an appreciation of the past. Thus, my third proposition deals with the past. We look to the past because it helps us to achieve the future.

My parents had a vision of the future in some respects but lacked it in others. Should I not avail myself of their experiences? I can either avoid the pitfalls they experienced, or perhaps I can discover how they were able to scale some of the heights they conquered. To ignore the past is to damn ourselves into repeating the whole experience.

It would be most unfortunate if our society should split itself into the "now" generation and the "has-been" generation. Every generation, somewhere in its history, senses that a particular moment, *now,* is more important for itself than any other moment. Yet every generation needs to be in touch with the generations which have gone before and the generations which will come afterward.

Americans seem to lack a sense of history. When the late Paul Tillich first came to America, he remarked that one of his first impressions of Americans was their lack of interest in the past. When a person attempts to teach church history to a group of junior highs, he soon realizes how strong is their feeling that if something doesn't exist now, it isn't real. All in all, we have little appreciation for the past. I recall in postwar Germany that a G.I. friend received a letter from his sister in a stateside college. He was urged to visit a famous ancient building in the town in which we were stationed. When he returned, I asked him what he thought of it. His response was, "If it had been in America, we would have torn it down long ago and put a filling station in its place."

The price of neglecting history is a tragic one, however. The United States has been deeply involved in Vietnam for many reasons, one of which is that it ignored the history of the Vietnamese people, the history of the French involvement in that country, and our own national history.

We have experienced many a long hot summer in America's cities because we have ignored our own history. We have never recalled, if we ever learned it, the long history of white exploitation of the blacks. We have ignored, if we were ever aware of, the history of Europe and her cities. We have ignored the history of our own political, economic, and social development.

As a nation we need to be aware of the realities of the past. More personally, as families we need to be more aware of our own family traditions. We need to recover some of the struggles, some of the dreams and aspirations of our forebears. What did they do? What did they do right? What did they do wrong? What did they do that possessed meaning for their day and ours?

Now, the present moment, is never enough if it stands isolated from the future and the past. I also believe that we can discover the significance of the present by relating it to the future. Toward what are we headed? What are our life's goals? What are our aims? What is our direction?

Once we have caught a vision of the future, we can turn to the past to better understand how best to go about winning the future. The lessons of the past can help us incorporate the future into the present.

The *now* can be every bit as much a tyrant as the past can be. The fresh possibilities of the future can liberate us from the tyranny of present and past. Whatever it is in either the past or the present that holds us in bondage, we have a glorious future in the liberty which Christ alone provides. Let us measure our future by the possibilities available in Jesus Christ.